SERIAL KILLERS

KILLERS

AT THE MOVIES

SERIAL KILLERS
AT THE MOVIES

CHRISTOPHER BERRY-DEE

First published in 2020 by Ad Lib Publishers Ltd
15 Church Road
London, SW13 9HE

www.adlibpublishers.com

Text © 2020 Christopher Berry-Dee

ISBN 978-1-913543-83-9
eBook ISBN 978-1-913543-77-8
ISBN 978-1-786751-17-1

A CIP catalogue record for this book is available from the British Library.

Every reasonable effort has been made to trace copyright-holders of material reproduced in this book, but if any have been inadvertently overlooked the publishers would be glad to hear from them.

Printed in the UK
10 9 8 7 6 5 4 3 2 1

Visit the author's
website @ www.christopherberrydee.com

DEDICATION

For writer Michael Eaton, director Roger Bamford, producer Nick Finnis, theme music composer Debbie Wiseman, and the cast and crew of *Harold Shipman: Doctor Death* (2002).

CONTENTS

INTRODUCTION

You just can't make this stuff up. Crime movies have been popular as long as movies have been around, and the world keeps providing ever-stranger real-life material for them to use. It'd be hard to invent the terrifying stories behind classics like Martin Scorsese's Goodfellas, *or more scuzzy works like the vacation-from-hell horror movie* Wolf Creek *and they didn't. In recent years, the 'based on a true story' conceit has become a tired Hollywood trope, but only because these movies so masterfully blended nonfiction with the wild imaginative possibilities of the big screen.*

Paul Schrodt, *Esquire*, 26 October 2017

Yes, I ate the pussy of that hooker. Had dumped the body over a bridge into a culvert ... went back a few days later and it was froze solid. Hacked the vagina out and thawed it under my car heater. Ate most of it and chucked the bone outta the window. Then I went to Dunkin Donuts and chatted with the cops there. Dumb fuckers, they were looking for me statewide and there I was in front of 'em.

Arthur John Shawcross, aka 'The Monster of the Rivers', to the author, Sullivan Correctional Facility, New York, on the murder of June Stott, aged thirty.
Monday, 23 October 1989

As anyone who watched Hannibal Lecter's brutal and merciless jailbreak in *The Silence of the Lambs* (1991) or the chilling dénouement in *Seven* (1995) will testify, there is something terrifyingly compelling about serial killers.

Their portrayal on the silver screen draws us into a world where we would otherwise dare not tread. The movies that best convey the psychological allure of the worst kind of evil in society stay with us long after the cinema lights come back on and we're home, safely tucked up in our beds.

What is it about the depraved, the deranged and the downright dastardly that provides such entertainment value? It is not only serial killers who capture movie fans' imaginations. Gangsters, robbers, con artists – the most evil living in society – whose notoriety comes at a human cost. Even the bungling criminally-minded fools make for enthralling characters that keep us coming back for more.

Why do we relish these gory screenings in glorious blood-drenched high definition with digital surround sound gunshot blasts, and bone-chilling screams? Is it simply that we subconsciously like to see others suffer as long as it is not us? Is there is a grim voyeurism attached to suffering, planted deep within our DNA? There is certainly something lurking within the most primitive part of our brains – often called the 'reptilian brain' – responsible for survival, drive and instinct, that thrives on the fight or flight mode. We are hard-wired to respond to shock and fear.

For as long as films have been made, right back to the silent movies of the early twentieth century, audiences have loved being thrilled. The first Western in recognisable form, *The Great Train Robbery* (1903), quickly established the essential formula of pursuit, showdown, followed by justice, while of course including fisticuffs, gunfights and, crucially, a daring heist. The film was only twelve minutes long but its power was palpable. People ducked when they saw the train coming on the big screen. Fast forward to 1991 and audiences were reportedly vomiting in the cinema aisles and asking to be escorted to their cars – so scared were they by Hannibal Lecter's fondness for flesh-eating. Not only were these movies linked by their propensity to shock, but also their subject matter. Since the beginning of time people have been fascinated by crime stories.

But from where does the inspiration for such grisly storylines come? *The Silence of the Lambs* was of course adapted from Thomas Harris's book of the same name. How could Harris dream up a character as sinister but compelling as Hannibal Lecter, someone who could joke about eating a man's liver 'with some fava beans and a nice Chianti'? Surely nothing in real life could be so gruesome as a psychiatrist who enjoys eating human flesh. Or, indeed, the psychotic serial slayer 'Buffalo Bill' he helps FBI agent Clarice Starling catch, who tortures and torments his victims. What about the sadistic killer we saw in *Seven*, who plots his murders around the deadly sins, manipulating the very detectives who are pursuing him.

Perhaps more terrifying than even these storylines and characters is the shocking truth that such twists are not purely plucked from the overactive imagination of a creative scriptwriter or novelist. Quite often, the inspiration comes from real-life criminals. As the old maxim states, truth is stranger than fiction. Whether it be a crime movie, a TV drama or a novel, somewhere in the plot will be an echo of wicked events drawn from real life. Many works of fiction are based upon some semblance of fact.

Real-life serial killers, as I have found in my many face-to-face interviews with them, are all about taking revenge. It is what makes them tick. In most circumstances, deep within the homicidal psychopath's flawed mindset, he – or she – is exacting some form of vengeance for a self-perceived wrong done to them in the past. He may harbour an overwhelming grudge against his mother whom he wants to kill but cannot, so he lets loose his hatred and discontent on other women who have done him no harm at all.

A perfect example of this was sadosexual serial murderer Ted Bundy, who was part inspiration for Harris's Buffalo Bill in *The Silence of the Lambs*. Bundy was someone who harboured a hatred for a certain victim type, just like his silver-screen incarnation. Jilted by his first true love he took out his homicidal rage on scores of young women who appeared to come from the same mould. Most of them were young co-eds; all were extremely attractive, most had long, dark hair; indeed, if one were to place all of their photographs side-by-side one might imagine they were sisters, which, more-or-less, they were – sorority sisters even.

Another was the wicked Edward Theodore 'Ed' Gein, aka 'The Butcher of Plainfield', someone so cold and evil he was the inspiration for not one iconic movie character but several, including Norman Bates in *Psycho* (1959), 'Leatherface' in *The Texas Chainsaw Massacre* (1974), as well as the aforementioned Buffalo Bill.

The real-life inspiration for some of Hollywood's most shocking movies – the criminals behind the characters, their scarcely believable crimes, their modus operandi and their comeuppance – is the basis for this book. It will also explore how these most heinous of events have been manipulated purely for the purposes of entertainment.

I seek to draw you into my world as an investigative criminologist, sharing some of my own personal experiences of when I've come face to face with the very same people who have provided this inspiration. I will direct you to material available online that will enhance your understanding of what have, in my opinion, been worthy representations of true crimes and those that are less so. I am no movie critic, but I believe I am qualified enough to determine which movies are worthy of study by true crime aficionados. And, while it's not an exhaustive rollcall of every crime movie, it should give some insight into how some notorious crimes slip into the world's collective consciousness, elevating evil perpetrators to near mythical status.

In other instances, the cinematic attempt to retell heinous acts of violence fails to do justice to some of the most horrendous episodes in criminal history. Sometimes a film's true crime origins are too prosaic to merit a full inclusion here, but that doesn't mean the movie isn't without merit. A perfect example is *Layer Cake* (2004), the British mystery thriller adapted by J. J. Connolly from his novel of the same name, which had all the right ingredients for a gripping movie. When Connolly came up with the concept of a cocaine dealer who wanted one last big deal before turning his back on a life of crime he based his main man – the mysteriously unnamed XXXX, played by Daniel Craig – on a number of criminals he'd encountered. Accurate research, a great cast, memorable locations and a tight plot was a recipe for success for director Matthew Vaughn and it launched Craig's career.

All too often, however, moviegoers have been conned into paying money for cinematic trash, as was the case with *The Amityville Horror*, released in 1979. Based on the dreadful real-life mass shooting of the DeFeo family at their home on Long Island, in November 1974, this film was a classic case of victim exploitation. I watched the film at the age of thirty-one unaware at that moment that, twenty years later, I would be interviewing the convicted mass murderer, Ronald 'Butch' DeFeo Jr, himself. The book on which the movie was based – by American author Jay Anson – was an utter amoral fraud, combining an imagined ghost story with the real-life tragedy. If the original movie was an affront to the memories of those tragic victims then what did that make the many excruciating sequels that followed? While movies based on true events are often produced with heart and soul, and not with a fast buck in mind, this rode roughshod over the memories of the dead.

We all like to be 'entertained', but filmmakers have a duty to produce responsibly made, well-researched motion pictures when they are basing them on real crimes. Told well, a movie can serve as a warning of the dangers that serial killers and mass murderers pose to us all. As discerning film fans, we can vote with our wallets and not endorse cheap flicks made purely to cash in on a case's notoriety. We should look at the messages behind the plots and watch and learn. One should never lose sight of the fact that behind every dramatisation of a real-life tragedy – however loosely the facts are presented – a real person, in an actual place, has met a truly terrible end.

I single out *Ruth Ellis: A Life for a Life* (1999) as the touchstone for every producer considering a movie about real-life murder. Ruth Ellis will forever be known as the last woman to be hanged for murder in Britain, following her conviction of the murder of her lover, David Blakely, on Easter Sunday 1955. Their relationship had been abusive. Utterly distraught, Ellis had waited for Blakely outside the Magdala public house in Hampstead, and when he came out she shot him five times using a .38-calibre Smith & Wesson revolver. She was hanged by state executioner, Albert Pierrepoint, at 9 a.m. on 13 July 1955.

Available to watch on YouTube, the BBC One drama documentary, narrated by Kirsty Wark, is very informative and thoroughly well researched, capturing perfectly the atmosphere of the 1950s. Running at fifty-seven minutes, the programme is as close as one can get to the truth about Ruth and her downfall. Featuring rare interviews with her former QC, and her solicitor, also with John Cooper, designer of the original Mini Cooper car, who happened to know both Ruth and Blakely, the programme is based upon official trial transcripts and police documents. It also includes disturbing post-mortem photographs of Blakely lying in the street and on the coroner's slab.

Fiona Ormiston gives a spectacular performance as Ruth. John Light (David Blakely), Julian Curry (Mr Justice Havers), Philip Dunbar (Christmas Humphries), Andrew Hilton (Melford Stevenson QC), along with a first-rate supporting cast, make this a stand-out production. It sets a benchmark, and goes to show what a great, eye-opening, highly controversial and dark true-life crime conversion for the TV screen, should be.

I appreciate it is a difficult task to capture in just one ninety-minute screening all the nuances, the aftermath and ramifications of a criminal enterprise but a host of moviemakers have shown it is possible. Take the case of John Reginald Christie, a serial killer who killed his wife, Ethel, and kept her corpse under the floorboards of his living room; three other female victims who were walled up in his kitchen; the corpses of a mother and baby that were tied up in sheets in the backyard outhouse that also served as a toilet; plus two corpses that he buried in the garden, right under where he grew his peas – all his victims disposed of in an area the size of a few hundred square feet. On the face of it, the number of corpses in such a confined space would make his conviction a foregone conclusion, yet a bungled police investigation meant that an innocent man, Timothy Evans, whose wife and daughter were among the victims, was hanged for their deaths.

Powerful and emotive, *10 Rillington Place* (1971) immaculately chronicles the real-life case, and the controversy of the false conviction which, together with the fury over the hanging of Ruth Ellis, eventually led to the abolition of capital punishment in the UK. Starring Richard Attenborough as Christie, John Hurt as Evans, and a great supporting cast that included Pat Heywood and Judy Geeson, it is a disturbing drama; one that deserves to be watched several times to appreciate the subtle cinematic nuances underpinning the screenplay. It is as close to the stories of John Christie and Timothy Evans as one can get.

It is not only skilfully executed dramatic treatments that link the cases of Ruth Ellis and John Christie. The hangman who presided over the sentences for both Christie and Evans was Albert Pierrepoint who was present at the execution of Ruth Ellis. Pierrepoint went on to be an advisor on *10 Rillington Place*, which only added to its authenticity.

Compare and contrast that movie with *Rillington Place* (2016), a TV drama covering the same ground with Tim Roth as the serial killer, Nico Mirallegro as Timothy Evans and Jodie Comer – coincidentally now modernising the concept of a serial killer for the twenty-first century as Villanelle in the hit BBC series *Killing Eve* – as his tragic wife Beryl. With such a solid cast you might expect a decent dramatisation but this three-parter doesn't hold a candle to the original 1971 movie, simply because the research for the original was so impeccable.

Highlighting cases where movies have fallen well short of the mark is another aim of this book and therefore, hopefully, it will provide a toolkit to help film fans sort the wheat from the chaff.

While movies have routinely drawn inspiration from true crimes, it is not always a one-way process. Sometimes life imitates art and real life mirrors some iconic moments on the silver screen. *Fatal Attraction* (1987), in which Michael Douglas' married attorney character, Dan Gallagher, bites off more than he can chew with Glenn Close in a career-defining role as unhinged book editor Alex Forrest, was born from scriptwriter James Dearden's real life experience. One weekend, while his wife was out of town, he contemplated calling a woman he'd met some months before. He didn't make the call but the idea of what might happen if he had and things turned nasty inspired him to write a short British movie called *Diversion* (1980). Later Paramount Pictures developed it into *Fatal Attraction*, which became the highest grossing movie of the year worldwide, and the term 'bunny-boiler' became synonymous with any obsessive, jilted woman. In 1992, at a second trial, twenty-eight-year-old teacher Carolyn Warmus was convicted of murdering forty-year-old Betty Jeanne Solomon, her lover's wife, in Greenburgh, New York. During the trial Betty Jeanne's husband Paul told the court Warmus had been upset when he broke off their affair, claiming, 'Life's not worth living without you.' The prosecution alleged that Warmus bought a gun and used it to kill Solomon's wife. The case became national news with media outlets calling it a real-life *Fatal Attraction* and it spawned a number of TV docu-dramas, completing the circle back to entertainment.

For every accurate portrayal of a real-life event there are times when Hollywood's take on the realities of certain vulnerable communities is laughable and verging on dangerous.

Take the Cinderella story, *Pretty Woman* (1990), in which Richard Gere's millionaire business-asset stripper, Edward Lewis, plucks Julia Roberts' down-on-her-luck streetwalker, Vivian Ward, from obscurity in Los Angeles and into a world of impossible wealth, glamour and romance.

Sadly, in reality, the only 'asset strippers' sex workers are in danger of meeting are the type of premeditated butchers who stalk their prey before abducting them, subjecting them to terrifying ordeals before dumping their lifeless bodies. Men like flat-cap-wearing, dirty-fingernailed kidnapper, blackmailer and killer Michael Benneman Sams, whom I interviewed many years ago in HMP Full Sutton. Habitual criminal and power tools salesman Sams picked up eighteen-year-old Julie Dart, a sex worker from Leeds, in July 1991. Instead of taking her to an upmarket restaurant like the plot of the movie, Sams took Julie to his warehouse, blindfolded her and placed her in a coffin-like box chained to the floor. He demanded a £140,000 ransom from her boyfriend but, before the money was paid, bludgeoned her to death with a hammer and dumped her body in a field in Lincolnshire.

In January 1992 he struck again, kidnapping estate agent Stephanie Slater after arranging to meet her at a property in Birmingham. This time the ransom was paid, and Stephanie escaped with her life after chatting to Sams for the eight days she was tied up, trying desperately to increase her chances of survival. Sams was later caught when his ex-wife recognised his voice from a police tape.

It is from covering gruesome cases like this and coming face to face with sadistic killers like Sams that I despair when Hollywood sells us unrealistic fairytales and when crimes are exploited. I understand that the nature of film and TV making is to provide entertainment. That's not necessarily a bad thing *if* they actually help us all understand the impact of real-life homicide and the human stories behind the crimes. For instance, any programme that educates the general public about the value of forensic science contributing to the apprehension of a killer is, in my mind, a must-watch. With the fascinating detail that shows like *CSI* go into, I'm always surprised when subsequent wannabee crooks fail to take heed of the valuable lessons they're being shown in how to avoid identification and capture. It just shows that very few are the masterminds they take themselves to be.

And so, with that in mind, all that's left for me to say is grab some popcorn, pour a chilled glass of something and settle down for a trip through the shocking true stories that have tantalised Tinseltown.

A word of warning – some of the content matter is not for the faint hearted. So, fittingly, as Bette Davis nearly said in *All About Eve* (1950), 'Fasten your seatbelts, it's going to be a bumpy ride!'

The Silence of the Lambs

A wily and intelligent criminal behind bars, a young visitor keen to glean some insight into a killer's psyche. However, instead of the eager inquisitor asking all the questions, it is the enigmatic inmate who is probing, playing, wanting his own ego stroked.

If this exchange sounds eerily familiar, that's because it could be a description of the scene from *The Silence of the Lambs* where Anthony Hopkins' serial killer psychiatrist, Hannibal Lecter, toys with nervous young FBI agent, Clarice Starling, played so brilliantly by Jodie Foster, as she hunts for a murderer. But this isn't a scene from the big screen – not originally, at least. It is in fact the moment when a mysterious doctor called 'Salazar', a real-life medic in prison for murder, met writer Thomas Harris, then a fledgling reporter working on a story for *Argosy*, an American pulp fiction magazine (published between 1882 through 1978). Harris was visiting another prison inmate, Dykes Askew Simmons, at the Topo Chico Penitentiary, Nuevo Leon, Mexico, in the 1960s. Having heard that Salazar had saved Simmons' life after he had been shot in the face trying to escape, Harris sought a meeting with the medic. He was invited to take a seat but soon found that the tables had turned as it was Salazar who began asking questions, deflecting attention but at the same time providing a small window into his complicated psyche. Salazar wanted to know how Harris had felt when he came face to face with Simmons? Had Harris noticed the disfigurement of Simmons' face caused by the shot to his face by the prison guard? Had he seen photographs of Simmons' victims? Did the sunglasses Simmons wore add symmetry to his face?

This real exchange and the unsettling effect it must have had on the young Harris – only twenty-three at the time – played a significant role in shaping the character of Hannibal Lecter, the human-flesh-eating psychopath who engaged and horrified cinemagoers in equal measure. But this is where truth ends and fiction begins, because by the time Salazar was re-imagined by Harris in the 1981 novel *Red Dragon* he was depicted as a brilliant psychiatrist and a cannibal, something the mysterious Salazar certainly was not.

Following the success of *Red Dragon*, it was no surprise Harris penned a sequel, *The Silence of the Lambs*, published to widespread acclaim in 1988. The movie adaptation of the novel, from director Jonathan Demme, hit cinema screens in the UK on 31 May 1991. Made with what now seems like a modest budget of £15.5 million ($19 million), the film became an international success, earning back its budget on its opening weekend in America and, at the time of writing, the movie has grossed more than £222.6 million ($272.7 million) with the meter still ticking and this does not include revenue from the sequels: *Hannibal* (£288 million), *Red Dragon* (£171 million), and *Hannibal Rising* (£67 million).

So, who was the mystery doctor 'Salazar' that left such an impression on Harris and inspired a novel and movie franchise based on a character such as 'Hannibal the Cannibal'? Diego Enrique Osorno, a prominent Mexican author and poet, wrote a 2013 article for *Vice* where he claims that he and his girlfriend found 'the real Hannibal Lecter'. He reveals that 'Salazar' was, in fact, Alfredo Balli Trevino, a surgeon and a convicted murderer. Trevino, while incarcerated, saved the life of Simmons when he was shot in the face and disfigured by prison guards while trying to escape. Simmons, from Texas, had been convicted in March 1961 of murdering three young members of the Perez Villagomez family in October 1959.

Police records show that Dr Trevino had only killed once in what is called a *crime passionnel*: where the perpetrator commits the act against someone because of a sudden strong impulse, such as in a sudden rage rather than with premeditation. On Friday, 9 October 1959, Trevino got into an argument over money with his lover – another doctor – Jesus Castillo Rangel. Some commentators believe that they had a lover's tiff when Rangel threatened to leave him. Whatever the case, it seems that Rangel slashed Trevino's throat with a screwdriver. In a furious retaliation, Trevino attacked Rangel, slashing his throat with a scalpel. Rangel bled out in a bathroom. Trevino then methodically sliced up Rangel's corpse, chopped it into pieces and stuffed the flesh and bones into a box, which he then took to his uncle's farm where a farmhand helped him bury it as 'medical waste'.

The police report into this gruesome homicide was complicated. It's probably closer to the truth that Trevino used some kind of anaesthetic to sedate Rangel, then injected an additional drug into the unconscious body and dragged it into the bathtub where he slit his lover's throat with a scalpel and drained the blood from his body.

The day after Trevino visited the farm, another labourer called the police, having witnessed the suspicious burial. Two Mexican officers, initially pretending to be patients so as not to arouse suspicion, approached Dr Trevino in his office. Trevino was accused of trying to bribe the cops – offering a pay-off that included a pharmacy that belonged to his father, as well as promising each officer a new car – in return for them dropping their investigation.

After his arrest, police tried to connect Trevino with other murders and disappearances in the area but were unsuccessful due to lack of evidence. His name has, as a result, been constantly intertwined with the name of another predator known as 'The Werewolf of Nuevo Leon' who picked up hitchhikers before murdering them, dismembering them and throwing pieces of their body from his car window as he drove around at night.

When Harris first met with Trevino he was convinced that he was actually talking to a real prison doctor until a warden whispered in Harris's ear: 'Hombre, you don't know who that is? The doctor is a murderer. As a surgeon, he could package his victim in a surprisingly small box ... he will never leave this place. He is insane.'

Once Harris learned of the doctor's background he was eager to interview him but was taken aback when

Trevino began questioning him. He was fascinated to know what Harris made of Simmons. It was from this conversation that the character of Lecter took shape.

What is startling is that photographs of Trevino show a remarkable likeness to Sir Anthony Hopkins as Dr Hannibal Lecter. Harris would later describe Trevino as '...a small, lithe man with dark red hair', who 'stood very still ... There was a certain elegance about him.' It transpired that Harris later gave the doctor the pseudonym 'Salazar' to protect his true identity when retelling this story. This was a wise move because, despite the warden's claims, Trevino's death sentence was commuted to a twenty-year sentence and he was released in the early 1980s. Maybe Harris didn't want to get sued, hence 'Dr Salazar' came into being.

Although consumed with guilt for the murder of his lover and now in a wheelchair, Dr Trevino continued to treat patients. He said: 'I don't remember how many years I have been a doctor. Now I take care of the elderly, like me, but honestly I don't remember. At first it was difficult but, with time, things improved. However, some days depression comes back. I paid for what I had to pay. Now I'm waiting for divine punishment.'

Trevino spent the last years of his life helping the poor and elderly, just as he had looked after other inmates while in prison. One Monterrey resident, Dr Alfredo Balli Montiel, told Kaya Burgess writing for *The Times* newspaper, in 2013, that unearthing what happened to Trevino was like 'looking for a ghost'. Two patients once treated by Dr Trevino in his twilight years had nothing but praise for him. He never charged them for his medical expertise. If they could scrape together a few pounds they would give it to him. 'He was a good person,' one added. It seems Dr Trevino deeply regretted his impulsive actions and was determined to spend his life trying to atone for that devastating mistake – something that could never be said of Dr Hannibal Lecter.

As tragic and grisly as Trevino's actions were the night he took the life of his lover, the question remains how this single, seemingly unextraordinary murder grew into two internationally bestselling books and a combined £748.6 million ($833.4 million) in cinema box office receipts.

Trevino was by no means a calculated killer. He might have made a desperate attempt to evade justice by offering the bribe, but police quickly established he was the prime suspect. In terms of notoriety, his crimes didn't even come close to those of a British doctor, Harold Shipman, who killed over two hundred of his patients between 1975 and 1998 before he was caught. Indeed, history is littered with stethoscope-carrying killers who have committed far worse deeds than Dr Trevino.

Trevino was a fascinating and sinister character in many ways, but he was not a serial killer. A crime of passion, which was certainly the case here, is almost always committed with lack of forethought or premeditation. Dr Trevino had clearly not considered what he would do with a dead body. Had he been as cold and calculating as the fictional Dr Lecter then surely he would have at least found another way to dispose of the corpse than drive to his uncle's farm and enlist the help of a farm worker to dig a shallow grave right in front of witnesses. Trevino hardly seemed to be the 'brilliant' doctor introduced by Harris in *Red Dragon*.

During my lengthy career interviewing and corresponding with thirty or so serial killers and many other types of murderers, I have met a few cannibals of sorts and wrote about them in my book, *Cannibal Serial Killers: Profiles of Depraved Flesh-Eating Murderers*. There is no evidence whatsoever that Dr Trevino had ever eaten human flesh.

It's also interesting to review the prison warden's comment to Harris that Dr Trevino was 'insane' and likely never to be released. I have visited more incarcerated, murderous psychopaths than most people and have grown accustomed to prison guards over exaggerating how dangerous an inmate might be. I imagine Dr Trevino was one of the high-segregation category prisoners, those for whom tight security is a must, who spend nearly every hour behind bars and, when not, they are shackled hand and foot while being moved around the facility under close escort. I've experienced similar several times when a guard or a warden has told me the prisoner I am about to meet is an 'animal' and will 'tear' my 'head off' if I misrepresent him.

One example was in September 1994, when I interviewed Ronald 'Butch' DeFeo Jr, of *The Amityville Horror* infamy. The warden at the Green Haven Correctional Institute, Stormville, New York, told my film crew and I that DeFeo was 'possessed by demons' and that 'my officers will only enter DeFeo's cell in threes. He is unpredictable and highly dangerous. They often suffer nightmares even after talking to him for a few moments. They often need counselling afterwards too.'

We entered with trepidation, not knowing what to expect. Imagine our surprise therefore when we met the scrawny, little, mass-murdering coward that DeFeo truly is. He was sitting, unshackled, on a wooden bench by the general visiting area. His opening words to me were: 'I've been fuckin' waiting for two hours for you. Who do ya think I am? I got better things to do.'

For the avoidance of doubt, a journalist doesn't simply walk into a high security prison to interview a highly dangerous inmate and then start chatting to all and sundry. One is given permission to talk to the prisoner on the visiting docket and *only* that prisoner. The only exception to this was when I was given complete access to inmates for a week in the supermax Washington State Penitentiary, in Walla Walla. On this occasion the Director of Prisons, Chase Riveland, had given me express authorisation to do this, and had overseen the unlocking of the entire population of Death Row so we could sit around on the tier, drink some Coke and eat candy while we chewed the fat. It was all very amicable, non-threatening and quite an experience.

Perhaps it was the nature of the conversation Harris had with Trevino that created the spark that was to become the articulate psychopath, Lecter? The very name that Harris selected for his character has a significant etymology. From Medieval Latin *lectura*, 'a past reading,' from Latin *lectus*, past participle of *legere* 'to gather, collect, pick out, choose,' is precisely what Dr Lecter did when methodically selecting his own victims and as he meticulously questions Clarice. Most of the killers I have met in real life have asked similar probing questions. Mostly they are being inquisitive purely for their own sick pleasure. Such characters nearly always follow up details of their own heinous crimes with something provactive like: 'Does this shock you, Christopher?' It is their way – because they are sexual psychopaths – of trying to impress me, to gloat about what they have done and exert some form of mind control over me. However, my blunt reply is always a simple, 'Not at all. Let's move on.' That spoils their fun. With only scant details of the conversation between Harris and Trevino available, it's hard to determine what really happened but my experience is that a lot of murderers are also great manipulators.

It can be easy to scoff at the idea that a largely unremarkable killer like Trevino could be inspiration to create someone as sinister as Hannibal. But, most likely, it was the mundane qualities about Trevino that made such an impact on Harris. His 'Hannibal' had to be someone people could relate to, could *like* even. He preserved the calm, inquisitive, quiet intelligence of Trevino and embellished it to such a degree as to be almost fantastical, while keeping it rooted in the very ordinariness of real life. And that's what makes Hannibal Lecter so chilling a character – that he could be walking among us. Perhaps all it took was the suggestion that Trevino was a 'werewolf' to plant a seed in Harris's brain. Once he had the perfect name, Hannibal, and the perfect rhyming psychological literary wordplay, he was able to breathe life into his creation. It is the idea of a cannibal that strikes a very uncomfortable discord in our own psyche.

Harris had his likeable psychopath and all he needed was his perfect counterfoil. Harris hit the spot with

Clarice Starling, the young FBI agent drafted in to glean from Lecter clues that would help the agency track the serial killer they called 'Buffalo Bill'. For me, Jodie Foster was perfectly cast as the capable, doe-eyed rookie tasked to get inside the head of the incarcerated monster by her mentor, FBI Behavioural Science Unit Chief, Jack Crawford, played by Scott Glenn. I sensed a *Beauty and the Beast* scenario being introduced here, which works so well in fiction. Even the name 'Starling' and the subject of lambs suggests innocence to us. Starling could not have looked more startled when put in front of the allegedly brilliant psychiatrist and heinous psychopath, Hannibal Lecter, for the first time. Even though he was behind a bulletproof screen at the secure mental hospital run by his nemesis, the sleazy Dr Frederick Chilton, played by Anthony Heald, *he* is the one able to get inside *her* head.

While the real-life inspiration for Lecter seemed to possess a conscience and was able to exhibit and feel genuine remorse for his one-off crime 'Hannibal the cannibal' is the polar opposite. Fully emerged criminal psychopaths have no conscience because, in place of a moral compass, there is a black hole. They are unable to feel any compassion at all for other human beings and they kill with the same lack of concern as one might swat a fly. Furthermore, they do not genuinely regret any of their dreadful crimes, rather they boast about what they have done and revel in the attention caused by their sins.

Harris and screenwriter, Ted Tally, who adapted the novel for the big screen, perfectly deployed what scientists have since termed 'psychocinematics' – the ability to suck us completely into their world to the point where we are psychologically affected by what we view on screen. It was some achievement, not least because both writers managed to do so while at the same time avoiding what German philosopher Friedrich Nietzsche said was a potential pitfall of studying such sinister characters. Nietzsche said: 'Whoever fights monsters should see to it that in the process he does not become a monster. And if you gaze long enough into an abyss, the abyss will gaze back at you.'

In the making of this movie, Harris, Tally and director, Demme, tapped deep into our innermost fears and nightmares: the Stephen King-style mental asylum where the totally deranged are housed whooping and screaming; the oily, self-opinionated, self-serving Dr Chilton; the unsettling soundtrack; the cold dungeon-like basement cell fronted by bulletproof plexiglass; and Dr Lecter, standing stock still and deathly silent while sniffing the air like a predatory beast. Perhaps this was just how Harris viewed Dr Trevino when they met – like Lecter – a man of impeccable taste; worldly-wise, well-travelled, born of wit, possessing an unpredictable and dark charm, with the ability to turn roundly evil in a heartbeat. Lecter is, in many ways, like the main character from Robert Louis Stevenson's *Dr Jekyll and Mr Hyde*, able to switch between the respectable and the evil effortlessly and without warning. As Stevenson's Dr Jekyll said of his alter ego, Hyde: 'If I am the chief of sinners, I am the chief of sufferers also ... it is one thing to mortify curiosity, another to conquer it ... you must suffer me to go my own way.' How well Stevenson understood the psychopathological mindset is shown in his words: 'With every day, and from both sides of my intelligence, the moral and the intellectual, I thus grew steadily nearer to the truth, by whose partial discovery I have been doomed to such a dreadful shipwreck: that man is not truly one, but truly two.'

There are more echoes of Stevenson's horror classic in the film with Harris's main antagonist. Perhaps even sicker than Lecter, is Jame Gumb, aka 'Buffalo Bill' – later 'Mr Hide', a subtle off-the-cuff nod towards *Dr Jekyll and Mr Hyde* – played by the creepy Ted Levine. In *The Silence of the Lambs*, Gumb is a serial killer who targets slightly chubby women with an aim to imprisoning them and murdering them so he can use their skin to make a 'woman suit' for himself. Harris draws upon Gumb's allegedly dysfunctional childhood and his utter hatred of his mother which later manifests in his confused sense of identity and self-hatred. Gumb hates women but he wants to become a woman. He is too psychologically disturbed to qualify for transgender reassignment surgery – hence the making of a 'woman suit' seems to be a valid option for him.

The homicide cops tasked with tracking Gumb down figure out his modus operandi (MO); he is skinning his victims – a different part of each victim so that he can make his suit bespoke. Historically, it was said that the real Buffalo Bill, William Frederick 'Buffalo Bill' Cody (1846-1917), once scalped a Cheyenne warrior. It with this in mind that one officer in the film suggests the moniker because Gumb 'skins his humps'.

Gumb also inserts a death's-head hawkmoth pupa into his victims' throats as part of his ritual. He is fascinated by the insect's metamorphosis, a process that he wants to undergo by 'becoming' a woman. All moths go through this process, but Harris chose his moth species carefully: death's-head fits perfectly. Interestingly, the pattern on the moth's back in the film's posters is not the natural pattern of a death's-head hawkmoth. It is, in fact, Salvador Dali's *In Voluptas Mors*, a picture of seven naked women made to look like a human skull. The scene where the discovery of the pupa is made is well-researched in terms of forensic entomology. By studying the insect larval stages, forensic scientists in the film are able to estimate the post-mortem index, any change in position of the corpse as well as cause of death.

Throughout the two books and films we see Dr Trevino metamorphosing like the death's-head hawkmoth pupae into a monster, Hannibal Lecter. But when it comes to Jame Gumb, Harris managed to up the ante. There is no single killer in history that can be said to be the inspiration for Jame Gumb. Harris created an amalgam of perhaps six real-life serial killers, all with different motives, rolled into one human predator.

One real-life serial killer that comes close might be Jerome Henry 'Jerry' Brudos (1939-2006). He was the main inspiration for the actor, Ted Levine, who played Gumb, who said he based part of his performance on Brudos. Cross-dressing serial murderer Brudos, aka 'The Lust Killer' or 'The Shoe Fetish Killer', was a giant of a man. Mentally unhinged, he was a necrophile who committed the murders of at least four women in Oregon between 1968 and 1969. He was the younger of two sons; his mother had wanted a girl the second time around, so she was, to say the least, unhappy with the result being another boy instead. She constantly belittled Brudos and physically and emotionally abused him throughout his formative years and well into his teens. From a young age, Brudos fetishised women's shoes and, as a teen, began to stalk local woman, eventually attacking them and stealing their shoes. At seventeen after a brutal attack on a young woman he underwent psychiatric evaluation where he was diagnosed with schizophrenia.

Brudos's first confirmed kill was that of a nineteen-year-old door-to-door encyclopaedia saleswoman called Linda Slawson. In January 1968 she knocked on his door and Brudos lured her into his basement while his very young wife and two children were there. He knocked Linda unconscious with a wooden plank then strangled her. He then dressed her in a variety of female underwear and shoes he had previously stolen in several rape and murder attempts, arranging her body in different poses. Brudos then used a hacksaw to cut off her left foot – which he kept in a freezer – to use later to model his collection of stolen high-heel shoes. He disposed of her body in the Willamette River.

In May of that year, Brudos kidnapped eighteen-year-old Karen Sprinkler at gunpoint from the parking lot of a department store. He was dressed in women's clothing. He took her to his garage where he forced her to model his collection of women's clothing whilst he took photographs. After raping Karen, he strangled her and hung her from a pulley by her neck for several days. Brudos raped the corpse on several occasions and cut off Karen's breasts in order to make plastic moulds. When he was finally finished with Karen he tied her body to a car engine and threw her into the same river where he had disposed of Linda.

Brudos made two more unsuccessful attempts to abduct women in 1968 before finally coming upon twenty-three-year-old Jan Susan Whitney on Tuesday, 26 November 1968. Susan's car had broken down on I-5. He offered to drive her to his home on the pretence of letting her call for a tow truck. Inside his car, he strangled Susan with a leather strap. He raped her post-mortem and again kept the body hanging from a pulley in his garage for several days. During this time, he dressed in women's clothes and underwear, photographed himself with the corpse, and had sex with the now decomposing body. He cut off one of Jan's breasts and made a resin mould of it which he used as a paperweight. To dispose of the body, he tied it to a length of railway iron then threw it into the Willamette River, along with Slawson's foot, which had since rotted.

On Wednesday, 23 April 1969, Brudos abducted twenty-two-year-old Linda Salee, again from a store parking lot. He took her to his garage where he raped and strangled her. Brudos then 'played' with the body but because he felt her breasts were 'too pink', he decided to not cut them off. Instead, he wired her up to the mains and passed an electric current through the body in an attempt to make it 'jump'. It didn't. After this, he tied his victim to a car gearbox and threw her body into the Willamette River where she would join the remains of Linda, Karen and Jan.

Although Brudos was clearly obsessed with women's clothing he never appeared to aspire to become a woman. Nor did he skin his victims to make a dress out of human flesh or target overweight women. That particular trait was the preserve of Edward Gein.

If the murders committed by Jerome Brudos fell short of the slasher macabre guaranteed to put bums on cinema seats, then Ed Gein (1906-1984) was a prime candidate to bolster box office receipts. This weedy little specimen inspired many writers because he fashioned trophies or keepsakes from the bones and skin of human corpses he exhumed at a local cemetery and from the two women he murdered. Gein even fashioned a female skin suit and several skin masks, along with a lampshade. But he didn't have any interest in moths. However, like Brudos, Gein was found to be criminally insane. Ed was remanded to the Mendota Mental Health Institute, where he was incarcerated for the remainder of his days.

Still not enough psychopaths to create a truly unique fictional psychopath like Jame Gumb? Let's add Theodore 'Ted' Robert Bundy (1946-1989) into the mix with his highly successful modus operandi where he would wear his arm in a sling and pretend to be in need of help and polite young women would happily offer assistance. This is the same dirty trick that Jame Gumb uses to kidnap his victims. We could also add in Gary M. Heidnik, who kidnapped and tortured six young women and held them prisoner in his basement as sex slaves.

Then there are smatterings of Edmund Emil Kemper III in Jame Gumb. Kemper harboured a deep grudge against his grandparents and killed them when he was a teenager 'just to see what it felt like'. He subsequently spent time in a mental institution but was released when he turned twenty-one. After that, it is thought that Kemper went on to kill eight more women between 1964 and 1973 culminating in the murder of his own mother. Dubbed variously by the media as 'The Co-ed

Killer', 'The Co-ed Butcher' and 'The Ogre of Aptos', at six foot and nine inches and with an IQ of 145, this real-life killer is certainly grist for any slasher-writer's mill. At the time of writing, he is a resident of the California Medical State Facility and his next parole hearing is in 2024.

One other serial killer springs to mind while I research the work of Thomas Harris. Readers of my books around the world now know a thing or two about real-life serial homicide and so know that dumping a corpse into a river, or fast-flowing stream, is a tried-and-tested means of getting rid of incriminating evidence. Gary Ridgway, also known as 'The Green River Killer', had not been identified at the time Harris wrote his novels. Ridgway dumped women's bodies in rivers and, like Gumb, inserted foreign objects into their corpses. Forensic (or medico-legal) entomology is the study of the insects associated with a human corpse in an effort to determine elapsed time of death. This fascinating subject was referenced to great effect in the movie with the death's-head hawkmoth scene and would have been a crucial practice in later tracking down Ridgway.

Now, my challenge to readers is this: watch the Hannibal movies and try and spot the subtle nuances throughout that hint toward real-life serial killers and their motives. Ask yourselves: 'What are the real-life crimes that inspired Thomas Harris to draw the characters in his books and movies?' Then think about the original conversation with Dr Trevino from whom this all sprang.

Finally, let's take a look at the other aspects of *The Silence of the Lambs* that show a commitment to authenticity which is almost criminally lacking in other movies I'll address in later chapters. To begin with, the real-life FBI's Behavioural Science Unit, Quantico, Virginia, were on hand to provide any assistance they could in the production of the film. Furthermore the movie was, in part, inspired by the real-life relationship between University of Washington criminology professor and former FBI offender profiler, Robert 'Bob' D. Keppel, and the serial killer Ted Bundy. While on death row, Bundy spoke at length to Keppel including offering help in profiling 'The Green River Killer' who was being hunted at that time. I highly recommend to the reader any of Keppel's books, amongst them being, *Signature Killers*, *The Riverman*, and *The Psychology of Serial Killer Investigations*.

So, you can see that the filmmakers accessed a wealth of real-life law enforcement and criminologist experience to support their production and creative teams. In addition to this, we have an actor with the dedication and integrity of Sir Anthony Hopkins bringing gravitas to the role of Dr Lecter. According to IMDB.com, Sir Anthony studied files of serial killers, visited prisons and researched convicted murderers. He was even present during court hearings concerning gruesome murderers and serial killings. Jodie Foster spent a lot of time with real-life FBI Agent, Mary Ann Kruse, prior to filming. Indeed, the amount of time, expense and effort that went into making *The Silence of the Lambs* as realistic and authentic as possible is hugely impressive.

In an online interview, published in 2019 by *New York Times Service* and written by Alexandra Alter, Harris is quoted as saying: 'I don't think I've ever made up anything ... Everything has happened. Nothing's made up. You don't have to make anything up in this world.' Alter is understandably disturbed by this idea. Perhaps Harris *is* gilding the lily a bit, nevertheless, for nearly forty-five years he has terrified audiences with his work, and his books have sold more than fifty million copies.

It is no surprise that the character of Clarice Starling was chosen by the American Film Institution as the sixth out of a list of fifty greatest movie heroes and the highest ranked female on the list. Dr Hannibal Lecter was chosen as the number one greatest movie villain – also out of a list of fifty – testament to the original writing, the screenplay, direction and acting that made this movie so powerful. And to think, it all began when the real-life Dr Trevino, in a moment of impulse, killed his lover, chopped him up and buried him in a box.

The Amityville Horror

The noun 'Amity' means friendly relations – peace, harmony and goodwill. All of which was turned upside down when Ronald DeFeo Jr blasted his family of six to death as they slept in their warm beds in their home in Amityville, Long Island, New York. A sleepy village in the town of Babylon, Suffolk County, one legend has it that the town was so named after bedlam broke out at a town meeting and one resident cried out 'What this meeting needs is some amity!' Another legend suggests that it was named after the boat of a local mill owner.

In recent years, Amityville's population has been just under ten thousand. Annie Oakley is said to have been a frequent guest of vaudevillian Fred Stone who lived there. Actor Will Rogers had a home there, as did gangster Al Capone. Actor Alec Baldwin and actress Christine Belford were both born in Amityville. British composer, Benjamin Britten, lived there for a while.

Then the DeFeos arrived in town.

DeFeo Sr was the service manager of a Buick car agency in Brooklyn and made a very good living. Real estate agent records show that on 28 July 1965, the DeFeos attained a trophy-sized piece of 'the All American Dream' – soon to be 'the All American Nightmare' – when they purchased a two-and-a-half storey, Dutch Colonial-style detached house from Joseph and Mary Riley, a couple who had lived there peacefully for decades without major incident.

Today, the exterior of 112 Ocean Avenue remains much the same as it did when the DeFeos moved in. It boasts its own swimming pool and a private dock backing onto a protected canal so by anyone's standards the house is prime real estate. But not everyone was happy when their new neighbours arrived in their quiet community. The DeFeos were loud and flashy. Curtains twitched and gossip started. Many of the locals became certain that Mr DeFeo had mob connections. DeFeo Sr was in fact the nephew of Peter DeFeo, a New York mobster who joined the Luciano crime family that operated in Lower Manhattan and Brooklyn. Certainly there were questions over how the family could afford such a house. Mrs Louise DeFeo, aged forty-two, was a gentle person and in her youth she had been enough of a beauty for modelling to be a prospective career. Together they had five children: Ronald DeFeo Jr (known as Butch), Dawn, Allison, Marc and John.

Almost as soon as they moved into 112 Ocean Avenue, forty-three-year-old Ronald Sr erected a sign in his grass-covered front yard that read, ironically, 'High Hopes'. The interior of the house was made even more flashy with its expensive furnishings, crystal chandelier and alabaster fireplace. In the early seventies, Ronald Sr commissioned life-size portraits of his family and these were hung in gold frames along the family staircase.

But if Mr DeFeo wanted to present a façade of domestic bliss to the outside world then the reality was quite different. Ronald DeFeo Sr was a physically imposing, hard man who ruled his family with an iron fist. He frequently had explosive fights with his wife and children. He demanded respect. Perhaps because he was the first born, Mr DeFeo was particularly hard on his eldest son. As a child, Butch was quite overweight and his school life was tough as other children picked on him. His father would also discipline him in the cruellest fashion. At trial, Louise's brother recalled an incident where Ronald Sr had pushed his son into a wall where he banged his head or shoulder in response to something quite unremarkable from the child.

Growing into a bully like his father, Butch hung around with a crowd of drug-addicts, alcoholics and general deadbeats. I've interviewed several of them and the effects of years of taking illegal drugs have taken their toll. Butch stole just about everything that wasn't nailed down, drove around Amityville burning rubber at high speed, was always involved in altercations and was accused by Ronald Sr of stealing money from a tin that had been hidden for safekeeping under the floorboards of the house.

For all of Mr DeFeo's sins, we can say that he was overly generous to his oldest son. He bought him cars and even found him easy work at the car dealership. But Butch was always skiving off, and, one time, even pocketed the staff's wages after being entrusted with collecting the cash from a bank – he told his father that he had been mugged.

His father soon realised that his son had stolen the money and sacked him on the spot. Shortly thereafter, in a final attempt to get his wayward child back on the straight and narrow and give him a healthy interest, he purchased the youth a speedboat and put the title in Butch's name. Young DeFeo promptly set the boat on fire then unsuccessfully tried to claim on the insurance.

By this time Butch had also acquired a couple of firearms – a 12-gauge shotgun and .35-calibre Remington Marlin martini-action rifle.

At some point in the lead up to the events of November 1974, police believe a violent fight broke out between Mr DeFeo and his wife, during which Butch intervened. This was a brave thing for the twenty-three-year-old to do because his father was almost twice the size of his eldest son. Butch produced his shotgun and rammed it into his father's face.

'Leave that woman alone. I'm gonna kill you, you fat fuck,' screamed Butch.

He pulled the trigger. 'CLICK'. But the gun misfired.

We will never know what was going through Mr DeFeo's head at that precise moment. It was lucky for him it wasn't a hundred lead pellets. However, this certainly dampened his rage. He froze and watched his son sullenly walk away. 'Touch my mother again,' snapped Butch, 'an' I'll blow your fucking head off while you sleep.' He ran to his car and sped off but, while this incident had not resulted in harm, a further confrontation was clearly imminent.

No one could have predicted the incident with the shotgun was a precursor for mass murder, but it certainly seemed to inspire in Mr DeFeo Sr something akin to a religious conversion. He became a devout Catholic and neighbours watched with curiosity and perhaps some bemusement as he started digging up his well-manicured front lawn and erecting religious shrines. Even more curiously, he was seen praying with his rosary beads in front of one of them – a shrine of St Joseph and the Christ child.

Despite this religious awakening, Butch became convinced that one day his father would exact his revenge on him. He festered, ruminated and then finally decided to blow his father away along with his entire family, too.

During the late evening of 13 November 1974, Butch, high as a kite on pot, went down into the basement living area. He was the only member of the family with his own room. His siblings all shared. At the time Dawn was eighteen, Allison was thirteen, Marc was twelve and the youngest, John, was nine. He sat on his bed and watched the star-studded movie *Castle Keep* – a 1969 Second World War romantic drama. By the time it finished the remainder of the DeFeo family were asleep in bed. Amityville was quiet that night but the sound of muffled gunshots and the barking of a dog would soon shatter that peace.

In my book, *Talking with Serial Killers*, I give a detailed account of the scene that met the police officers in the early hours of the next morning, much of which comes from the mouth of Ronald DeFeo himself. The details of the crime scenes drawn from Suffolk County Homicide Police records make for grim reading.

In the master bedroom, Ronald DeFeo Sr, had been shot twice in the lower back. The bullets went through a kidney and the spine. One stopped in the neck and the other ploughed through his body and into the mattress. At the autopsy, the medical examiner, Dr Howard Adelman, determined that death was most likely instantaneous since he was still on the mattress and it did look like he had tried to crawl out of bed.

Sleeping next to her husband, Louise had also been shot twice. The gunfire that had killed her spouse seemed to have awakened her, as she was turned in bed towards the doorway, the direction from which the shots had been fired. The first bullet entered her back, exited through her left breast and went through her wrist before stopping in the mattress. The second bullet destroyed her right lung, diaphragm and liver. Death most likely occurred in a matter seconds, since there are no signs that she put up a struggle.

Marc DeFeo and John DeFeo had each been shot in the back once. From the evidence, the medical examiner determined that their killer stood less than two feet from the boys when he discharged the rifle. Bullets penetrated the heart, lungs, diaphragm and liver of each victim. In addition, John's spinal cord was severed.

Allison DeFeo had been shot once. Like her mother, she had probably awakened and turned her head towards her bedroom doorway. The bullet smashed upward from her left cheek to her right ear, entering the skull and brain. The bullet exited, hitting the wall and bounced on the floor where it came to rest. Death was instantaneous, and powder burns on and around Allison's eyes indicated that she was awake at the time of her murder and staring down the barrel of the rifle.

Dawn DeFeo had also been shot once. Her older brother had stood less than three feet away and fired at the back of her neck. The bullet entered the left ear and collapsed the left side of her face. Brain particles splatted the pillow and the sheets were covered with blood.

It is obvious that Mr DeFeo Sr (who kept a loaded pistol in a drawer in the room where his body was found) was the first to be killed because he posed the biggest threat to the killer. Next had to be Mrs DeFeo for the gunfire in the master bedroom would have certainly woken her.

The weapon used in the slayings – the .35-calibre Remington Marlin 336C martini-action/lever-action rifle – is one of the choice rifles for taking down deer, bear, elk and even moose. Most .35-calibre rounds travel at around 2100 feet per second and this load generates circa 1900 pounds of energy. To get a sense of the power of this rifle and the noise it generates, look up 'Marlin 35 Remington Range 2' on YouTube and then imagine these shots being fired at point-blank range into sleeping humans inside a relatively small house at night.

The slayings were so cold-blooded it prompted Dr Adelman, deputy chief medical examiner of Suffolk County, to initially conclude from the evidence that this was a gangland-style execution. He surmised, wrongly, that at least three or four people had to have been involved and that at least two firearms were used – one being a pistol or a revolver maybe. It had to have happened this way, Dr Adelman said, because someone had to control the soon-to-be victims as they would surely have been woken by the sounds of gunfire.

Furthermore, DeFeo later told cops it was a mob hit on his father and that a gangster named Louis Falini held a grudge against him.

'I had an argument with Falini,' DeFeo told Detective Gozaloff. 'I called him a cocksucker and that caused problems between him and my father.'

But Dr Adelman's theory would hold no water at all because the forensic ballistic evidence would prove that all of the spent bullets found in the victims' rooms had all been fired from Butch's Marlin rifle.

When first spoken to by the police, Butch pledged his full cooperation and agreed to go to the First Precinct, calling beforehand at the Amityville Police Station to complete the paperwork that relieved the Amity Police of jurisdiction over the massacre. Over the course of the next forty-eight hours, Butch was questioned while in protective custody – with the initial worry being that Falini would soon come after him.

DeFeo was hardly a criminal mastermind, however, and his story started to come unstuck. At 2.30 a.m. on 15 November, Detective John Shirvell conducted a final sweep through the DeFeos' house. The rooms where the murders had taken place had been scoured thoroughly, but Butch's basement room had, up until that point, been given only a cursory once-over. Detective Shirvell found two empty rectangular boxes, each with labels describing their contents as .22-calibre and .35 calibre Marlin rifles. Although at that time he was still unaware that a .35-calibe rifle would be confirmed as the murder weapon, he took the boxes anyway in the event that they may become important evidence later.

Bit by bit, the detectives rubbished DeFeo's story, then Detective Dennis Rafferty and Lt Robert Dunn turned up. Eventually, having given Butch every chance to come clean, with their patience exhausted, the two cops ripped into him, even hitting him over the head with a Long Island telephone directory. DeFeo caved and told the cops exactly where the Marlin rifle was – in the dock behind his house where he had thrown it.

DeFeo is not a clever man. When I interviewed him in prison, he insisted that it was his sister Dawn who had killed the others but when she pointed the gun at him he took it off her and shot her in self-defence. This claim was not remotely believable, as Dawn was shot in her own bed, not rampaging around the house like someone possessed.

Face to face with him, I showed DeFeo a copy of the map he had drawn and signed. 'The Marlin was found by the police after you drew this map for them to show them where you threw the rifle,' I said. 'Look, that's your signature, isn't it, Ronnie?'

'No!' he said. 'The cops found the rifle themselves and then they drew the map but had asked me to sign that when it was a blank piece of paper first.'

More recently, there has been a heated debate about the rusty remnants of a revolver discovered deep in mud in the dock behind the murder house by a TV documentary maker and local divers. It has been hypothesised that this revolver was one of the firearms used by one of the accomplices – harking back to Dr Adelman's initial flawed theory. The simple fact of the matter is that the make, calibre or model of this weapon cannot be determined by forensic ballistic experts.

Neither can we begin to ascertain who may have owned it, fired it or even *when* it could have been thrown in the dock – although it is fair to say that this is close to where the Marlin rifle was found.

Having reviewed the ballistic reports and handled the bullets and spent shell casings myself, I can confirm – as did ballistic examiner, Detective Sergeant Della Penna – that the powder residue found at each murder scene was partially burnt particles of nitrocellulose gunpowder. The spent lead-jacketed bullets were of .35-calibre Remington Arms manufacture, originally being components of Western Co. .35-calibre cartridge cases.

What also isn't subject to debate is that Marc, John, Allison and Dawn would have been awakened by the sound of shots and would have lain in bed terrified before their eldest brother walked into their bedrooms and callously killed them. It was generally agreed that the shootings took place around 3.45 a.m. and, from start to finish, would have taken little more than ninety seconds to complete because five of the victims, Mr DeFeo, Mrs DeFeo, Allison, Marc and John, all slept on the same floor of the house. After killing them, Butch merely had to dart up a short flight of stairs to kill Dawn and complete his murderous rampage.

Most people when they sleep go through three stages. The first phase, when your eyes are closed, but it's easy to wake up, may last for five to ten minutes. The second is a light sleep, when the heart rate slows and your temperature drops as the body prepares for sleep. The third stage is deep sleep, when it's harder to rouse and, if suddenly woken, you would feel disorientated for at least a few minutes. Given the hour, it is likely that the DeFeos were all in this last stage of sleep when the killings began. This is a matter that Dr Adelman completely overlooked and something not mentioned in any of the subsequent literature produced in the years after the Amityville murders.

Ronald DeFeo Jr went on trial for the murders of his parents and four siblings in October 1975. By 21 November he had been found guilty on all six counts and was sentenced to six concurrent sentences of twenty-five years. He remains incarcerated at the Sullivan Correctional Facility in New York, which was where I interviewed him in 1994.

It is worth noting that, prior to the dreadful event that struck down the DeFeo family, there had never been any suggestion that 112 Ocean Avenue was haunted, either by a long-dead Indian chief, or a poltergeist or anyone else.

John and Catherine Moynahan had built the house in 1924 on semi-reclaimed land which means that if you dig down a little too far you will hit water. Not necessarily an ideal place for any ancient burial grounds. They and their children lived happily there for many years. The next owners were the Rileys, who described the house as 'airy, calm and spacious' and they had been reluctant to sell up, but personal needs necessitated it. There was not a bad vibe in the house until the DeFeos moved in. Prior to the murders there was never any mention, by anyone – least of all real estate agents or the local health authority – of green slime pouring down walls or out of taps, infestations of flies, a demonic, black-coloured pig with glowing red eyes called 'Jodie' flying around outside the windows, let alone a walled-up basement with a fiery Devil incarnate lurking behind the bricks.

Following the murders, the Lutz family moved in and actually lived peacefully on the property with their kids until they, in turn, sold it. Thereafter, ever since and right up until the time of writing this book, not so much as a cup has been dropped or thrown across the room by an unseen hand with subsequent owners always being delighted with their home on Ocean Avenue.

In 1979, just four years after the horrific night in Amityville, a new release hit cinemas with the tagline: 'George and Kathy Lutz moved into 112 Ocean Avenue in December 1975. Twenty-eight days later, they fled in terror.'

The film was based on a novel by Jay Anson called *The Amityville Horror*. Touted as a work of 'non-fiction' and 'the total truth', the book purports to relate the day-to-day events that drove the new residents of High Hopes from their home in abject terror. 'Their fantastic story, never disclosed in full, makes for an unforgettable book with all the shocks and gripping suspense of *The Exorcist*, *The Omen* or, indeed, *Rosemary's Baby*, but with one vital difference … the story is true!' reads the back cover.

The initial idea for *The Amityville Horror* was said to have initially come out over a few bottles of wine, when the attorney William E. Weber – while defending the killer Ronald DeFeo Jr – met up with George and Kathleen Lutz and between them they cooked up a story that shocked the world. They would claim that the property was haunted. It was possessed by the evil spirit of a long-dead Shinnecock Indian because High Hopes had been built on an ancient Indian burial ground. The book became a runaway bestseller and was made into the horror movie starring Rod Steiger, Margot Kidder and James Brolin.

The Lutz family's story of their time at High Hopes thrust Amityville and 112 Ocean Avenue into the world's spotlight once again. For forty-five years, the house has held the world in a grim fascination that reached beyond the tragedy of what happened to the DeFeo family. Eventually the notoriety the Lutzes had invited paid them back. Pestered by sightseers and turned into pariahs in their own community, they were forced to move out. On 30 August 1976, they returned their home to Colombia Savings and Loan. But it was not a haunting that made the Lutz family flee in terror – it was their own recklessness in trying to exploit a dreadful mass murder.

Like the story of the DeFeo family, the partnership between the Lutzes and Weber did not end happily. Once the Lutzes realised how much money was involved, they decided to cut Weber out of the deal. However, he had worded his contract with the Lutzes as we might expect an unscrupulous lawyer to do. He made off with the rights to the film then blew the Lutzes out of the way. He filed a lawsuit in the US District court in Brooklyn, presided over by Judge Jack B. Weinstein. In his decision, the Judge stated, '... the canons and ethics of law prevent Mr Weber from being involved in Mr DeFeo's criminal case and his appeals, while at the same time being involved in movie deals, books etc...' As a result of this ruling, Weber had to settle for a small amount of money out of court but it did not prevent him taking $20,000 from

DeFeo's relatives for appeals of the conviction. Nor did it stop him from finding other ways to profit from the Amityville tragedy. He teamed up with Professor Hans Holzer, an Austrian-American ghost-hunter. Together, they wrote a book called, *Murder in Amityville*, which, subsequently became the motion picture, *Amityville II: The Possession*.

Kathleen Theresa Lutz died of emphysema on 17 August 2004, aged fifty-eight. George Lee Lutz died of heart disease on 8 May 2006, aged sixty. The couple had divorced in the late 1980s but remained on good terms, still continuing to exploit their fictional account for money.

What a morbid exploitation of a real-life mass murder *The Amityville Horror* and all of the sequels truly are. It is akin to desecrating the graves of the dead and upsets me deeply. I sometimes wonder whether, if some of these exploitative filmmakers had lost a loved one under such terrible circumstances and viewed the broken body in a morgue, they would have been so quick to exploit the deaths of others.

The DeFeos met a terrible end but their memories were then slaughtered again by book writers, filmmakers and hordes of *Amityville Horror* fans ever since. It is shocking to see how the movie industry has financially milked one of the most notorious acts of familicide in history with a franchise that has lived longer than many:

1979: *The Amityville Horror* – writer, Sandor Stern.
1982: *Amityville II: The Possession* – writers, Tommy Lee Wallace and Dardano Sacchetti.

1983: *Amityville 3-D* – writer, William Wales.

1989: *Amityville 4: The Evil Escapes* – writer, Sandor Stern.

1992: *The Amityville Curse* – writer, Tom Berry.

1993: *Amityville: A New Generation* – writer, John Murlowski.

1996: *Amityville Dollhouse* – writer, Joshua Michael Stern.

2005: *The Amityville Horror* – writer, Scott Kosar.

2011: *The Amityville Haunting* – writer, Geoff Meed.

2013: *The Amityville Asylum* – writer, Andrew Jones.

2015: *Amityville Death House* – writer, John Oak Dalton.

2015: *The Amityville Playhouse* – writers, John R. Walker and Steve Hardy.

2016: *Amityville: Vanishing Point* – writers, Dylan Greenberg Selena Mars and Jurgen Azazel Munster.

2016: *The Amityville Legacy* – writers, Dustin Ferguson and Michael Johnson.

2016: *The Amityville Terror* – writer, Michael Angelo.

2016: *Amityville: No Escape* – writer, Henrique Couto.

2017: *Amityville: Evil Never Dies* – writer, Dustin Ferguson.

2017: *Amityville Exorcism* – writer, Billy D'Amato.

2017: *Amityville Prison* – writer, Brian Cavallaro.

2017: *Amityville: The Awakening* – writer, Franck Khalfoun.

2018: *Amityville: Mt Misery Road* – writer, Chuck Morrongiello.

2018: *The Amityville Murders* – writer, Chuck Morrongiello.

There are plenty of real resources readers can access to learn more about the true story. For those who have the stomach for viewing shockingly gross real-life scenes-of-crime photos many can be found online – but be prepared for sleepless nights. There are also countless books written about the murders and some include astonishing new information about the case.

My friend and colleague, director and writer Ric Osuna, wrote a book, *The Night the DeFeos Died: Reinvestigating the Amityville Murders*. And what a damn fine book it is. During his investigation into the Amityville murders, Osuna discovered a roll of film in a box at the Suffolk County Police HQ, in Yaphank on Long Island. Further investigation proved that this particular roll was part of a numbered, unbroken sequence of crime scene photos taken shortly after the police had arrived at High Hopes. The photographer had been down to the basement where Butch DeFeo slept and pan-shot the entire room, click after click. These photos of Butch's bedroom and his pool table are available to view online. Some of these photos were included as evidence at DeFeo's trial. After that they were sealed and stored at the police HQ where they remained, undisturbed, until Ric Osuna found them.

Upon closer scrutiny of the photographs taken of Butch's bedroom, Osuna saw something he'd not expected. The negatives showed clear images of something more terrifying than any fictional crime writer could invent. DeFeo's patterned sofa bed could be seen up against a wood-panelled wall in some of the photos used in evidence. However, in the photos discovered by Osuna is a different bed, almost Victorian in design. It is in exactly the same place as the sofa bed and behind it, running around the room, is wooden panelling. There is no pool table present and no TV, but it appears to be the same room. And on that Victorian-style bed is a dead body.

The body is that of a young girl, perhaps around the age of Allison DeFeo. She is wearing a nightdress. This mystery girl also appears to have been shot in the head. She is lying there, in exactly the same position as Allison was found. The trauma to both deceased girls' head is exactly the same, and the blood trails from the headshots are exactly the same too.

The wood panelling in the basement was tan in colour but in the mystery photos it is black. However, a much closer examination of the wood grain – which is like a fingerprint and unique in every respect – the knots and patterns appear the same. There can be no debate about this at all. This is simply fact.

There are other identical features in the two photos that prove beyond any doubt that these mystery photographs, which later 'self-developed' on a roll of police film, are of the same basement room. So, who was this mysterious dead girl? It is a question almost too terrifying to ask.

Ric and I worked on an in-depth, forensic examination of the mass murder while I was Director of the Criminology Research Institute (CRI). I had visited the police headquarters in Suffolk County before where I examined all of the exhibits, including the murder weapon, the Marlin rifle, bloodstained clothing, cartridge casings and the like. And I had also interviewed the primary case officers, Rafferty and Lt Dunn. One can find my videotaped interviews with these cops and DeFeo himself, and others online.

But in my investigations, I had missed the roll of film and Ric Osuna had not. He subpoenaed the Suffolk County PD and the film was released to him, and then to me. That's when we discovered those mysterious, unexplained images that were more terrifying than all of the crazy and twisted book and movie plots combined. What we saw was chilling. These photographs had been in police possession and they tried to keep them hidden away. Was what Ric and myself seeing the real-life supernatural captured on a roll of film?

Again we must see that the truth is often more fantastical than fiction. The case of the DeFeo family massacre was and is shocking enough without the fantasy added. It comes down to this – imagine that the DeFeo family were your loving kith and kin and imagine that their deaths were embellished for entertainment not just once but time and time and time again until the reality of what happened to them is almost indistinguishable from the myth.

Even the house has had to hide from the movie hype. On 18 March 1977, Jim and Barbara Cromarty bought the house for a mere $55,000, quite unaware of its infamous reputation. When they learned about its recent history, they were forced to change the address to 108 and add a fake window to the front of the building. Despite that, they were determined as they were to make their home part of the community again, but the Cromartys were bombarded with hordes of tourists looking for ghosts and demons. Eventually, the fans proved unbearable – they put the house on the market and moved out.

The Cromartys left a caretaker, Frank Birch, to tend to the property and act as house-sitter while they were away. It should be noted that neither Mr Birch nor the Cromartys ever reported supernatural occurrences. The family eventually moved back in and took the house off the market. They remained there until 1987.

On 17 August 1987, Peter and Jeanne O'Neil purchased 108 Ocean Avenue for an unspecified amount. They lived happily there until 1997, when they were forced to sell the place because of the high taxes associated with the property. According to friends, they chose to spend the money on their children's college education, rather than give it to the tax collector.

On 10 June 1997, Brian Wilson bought the house for $310,000. He resided there with his wife and two children, who attended college. He said that he was very happy with the house and had no complaints. In fact, he invested into the property by restoring the boathouse and improving the accommodation.

Caroline and David D'Antonio bought the 5000 square foot home in 2010 for $950,000. David passed away in 2015. In February 2017, 108 Ocean Avenue was sold to an undisclosed buyer for $605,000, which was $200,000 less than the original asking price. Broker Joanne Mills, who worked on the 2010 sale, said, 'The home's fame is both a plus and a minus as you might expect,' adding: 'It is an absolutely gorgeous five-bedroom, three-bathroom home and it's completely finished from top to bottom. The present owners [the D'Antonios] did even more refurbishment to the home and did a beautiful job. The home is haunted, yes, but not by who you think. It's haunted by the curiosity seekers that make it difficult for the people who live there.'

At the time of writing the valuation for the house is in the region of $800,000, which might be construed as a deal of a lifetime. 'It's a price to die for!' wrote an Amityville blogger, and who could argue? But would you want to live there?

The Texas Chainsaw Massacre

It's a familiar story – a group of dim-witted youngsters venture out into the middle of nowhere, run out of gas and end up systematically hunted down and butchered at a grim, isolated location. It feels like a tale as old as time, or at least as old as independent slasher flicks.

That it feels like such a well-worn movie trope is down to one film. *The Texas Chainsaw Massacre* achieved cult status and from a modest production budget of a mere £113,000 ($140,000) the film has grossed £25 million ($30.9 million) in receipts at the time of writing. Its success had little to do with a killer script – if you'll excuse the pun – or memorable acting. A key element of the buzz that built up around the film's release was how it was marketed. 'What happened is true', the film's promotional poster said. Another significant factor in the film's success was that, not long after the movie's release, it was banned in several countries after complaints about the gratuitous violence. Few things peak an audience's curiosity than being told it's not only a true story but it's too scary for cinemas.

In the film, Sally Hardesty and her wheelchair-bound brother, Franklin, travel to the site of their grandfather's grave to investigate reports it had been vandalised along with their friends, Jerry, Kirk and Pam. Somehow the group accidentally stumbled upon a family of crazed cannibals. We were introduced to 'Leatherface' and an iconic horror movie villain was born. Few characters have spent so much of their limited screen time doing so much damage. Only when it is too late do the youngsters realise they should never have approached the mysterious farmhouse in the woods to ask for gas. Who could have guessed that a psycho with a power tool – manically played to perfection by Gunnar Hansen – was lying in wait?

Quickly a legend sprang up around the film. Rumours circulated that there was an actual chainsaw-wielding madman living with his deranged family in Poth, a small town with a population of just two thousand in Wilson County, thirty-six miles southeast of San Antonio. The events that inspired the movie were said to have taken place in August 1973. The slight snag in this theory was that the film had already been shot by this time, but why let the facts get in the way of a good rumour?

The actual concept for *The Texas Chainsaw Massacre* came from the mind of an assistant film director at the University of Texas, Austin, Tobe Hooper, who said he intentionally misled audiences about the film's veracity as a response to being 'lied to by the government about things that were going on all over the world', including the Vietnam War, Watergate and the 1973 oil crisis.

Like *The Amityville Horror*, however, another big motivating factor must have been that they knew that telling people the story was based in truth would attract bums to seats. But they were, of course, stretching the truth. The movie was shot in Texas, at least. The setting for the 1900s house of horrors is located in Kingsland, Texas, in the grounds of the Antlers Hotel. So that much is true. But there were other elements of the movie inspired by real-life events.

Hooper used a cast of relatively unknown actors drawn mainly from central Texas, where the film was shot. The limited budget forced Hooper to film for long hours, seven days a week, so that he could finish as quickly as possible and reduce equipment rental costs. Due to the film's violent content, Hooper struggled to find a distributor, but it was eventually acquired by Louis Perano of Bryanston Distributing Company. Hooper limited the quantity of onscreen gore in hopes of securing a PG rating, but the Motion Picture Association of America (MPAA) rated it R. The film faced similar difficulties internationally.

Despite those early setbacks, it has since gained a reputation as one of the most influential horror films and the use of power tools as murder weapons has been much copied, as was the fascination of having a killer as a large, mute, relentless, faceless figure. Like *The Amityville Horror*, it led to a franchise that continued the story of Leatherface and his family through eight different sequels, prequels and a remake.

As it was, so much hype had built up around the movie's violence that many people might have felt short-changed when they actually witnessed the action. For much of the movie is spent following Sally Hardesty, her paraplegic brother Franklin, and their friends, Jerry,

Kirk and Pam as they visit the grave. A plot device that is very likely a nod to Gein's grave robbing and another connection to the case.

After visiting the grave, the youngsters decide to visit the old Hardesty family homestead and, along the way, they pick up a hitchhiker. The hitchhiker talks about his family who worked at an old slaughterhouse. He starts to behave strangely, tries to demand money for a picture he took of Franklin, then slashes the boy's arm when the others refuse to pay. When they kick the hitchhiker out of their van they probably hoped that was the last they'd see of him – but aficionados of horror movies know different.

The gang stops at a gas station to refill their van, but the owner tells them the pumps are empty. As they kill time waiting on the fuel delivery, Franklin mentions a swimming spot and Kirk and Pam go off to find it. That's when they stumble upon a spooky, rundown house. When Kirk enters with the intention of asking any occupants if they have some gas, a brute wearing a mask appears and, without warning, kills Kirk with a hammer. When Pam goes to investigate she finds a room filled with furniture made from human bones – another nod to Gein's ghoulish trophies. She tries to flee, but Leatherface grabs her, skewers her on a meat hook and makes her watch as he butchers Kirk with a chainsaw. As if that wasn't horrific enough, she is then removed from the hook and put in a freezer with all the implications being that she will be eaten later. Next Jerry goes looking for the others, finds the house and makes the chilling discovery of Pam, still alive, inside the freezer. Before he can save her, however, Leatherface pounces and kills him.

It's now left to Sally and Franklin to find what happened to their friends. No sooner do they arrive at the house when Leatherface appears and kills Franklin with the chainsaw. Sally runs inside and finds what seems to be the remains of an elderly couple. She manages to escape the house but, in true horror movie fashion, it's not that easy and ends up back in the clutches of Leatherface and the hitchhiker, who turns out to be his brother. Just as Sally fears she's about to become dinner for the messed-up family she manages to flee again and leaves Leatherface flailing around with the chainsaw in frustration.

'Leatherface' was so called because he sports a mask made of human skin. This, of course, has echoes of the real-life serial killer Edward 'Ed' Theodore Gein (1906-1984) also known as 'The Butcher of Plainfield' and the 'The Plainfield Ghoul'. Indeed, Hooper's co-writer, Kim Henkel, studied Gein before working on the script.

It's not hard to see why Gein provided good source material. He was a reclusive loner whose parents subjected him to serious psychological and physical abuse. His father, George, was a volatile, jobless alcoholic, while mother Augusta was a religious fanatic who preached the Old Testament and instilled in Ed and his brother, Henry, a fear of God and a distrust of women, telling them they would never be loved. Former classmates remembered Gein as having some strange habits, one of which was randomly laughing out loud as though told a hilarious joke that only he could hear.

By 1945, George had died from heart failure and Henry had lost his life in a mysterious house fire, which locals believed Ed had played some part in. When his mother also died that year Ed was devastated and, consumed by grief, boarded up her room in their secluded farmhouse to preserve it the way it was on the day she died.

Alone now in the house, Ed confined himself to a small room off the kitchen where he obsessed about the Nazis and cannibals. In November 1957, following the disappearance of Bernice Worden, a hardware store owner, a Waushara County Sheriff's deputy began to suspect Gein, who had been the last person to see her alive. He conducted a search of the Gein family home and made a grim discovery. He found Bernice – or what was left of her.

Bernice's decapitated body was hanging upside down inside the barn. The corpse was hung by its legs with a crossbar at her ankles and ropes at her wrists. The torso had been dressed out like a deer. A subsequent autopsy showed that the cause of death was instantaneous – with a .22-calibre rifle bullet going clean through her head.

The grisly discovery prompted a thorough search of the property and police were shocked to find that was only the tip of the iceberg. What they unearthed was enough to turn the stomach of even the most hardened detective. Among their discoveries were whole human bones and many fragments of the same; a wastebasket made from human skin; chairs also covered in skin; two human skulls on Gein's bedposts; sundry female skulls, some with the crowns sawn off and used as bowls.

The element of Gein's crimes that seems to have most inspired the character of 'Leatherface' was the grim discovery that Gein had used human skin to make a range of clothing. He'd fashioned a corset made from a female torso skinned from shoulders to the waist, human skin leggings and even a belt made from female nipples. And, in a find that would eventually lead to a multi-million-pound movie franchise, police discovered masks made from the skin of female heads. But that wasn't all. Among Gein's other prized possessions were a young girl's dress; the vulvas of two females judged by the medical examiner to be about fifteen-years-old; a shoebox containing a further nine vulvas; four noses; a pair of incised human lips attached to a window shade drawstring; a lampshade carefully crafted from the skin removed from a human face and fingernails from Ed's victims.

Investigators eventually found the remains of Bernice's head in a burlap sack and her heart in a plastic bag by the front of Gein's pot-bellied stove, all ready for cooking. As cops began to piece together what Gein had been up to they realised he had been exhuming corpses from local graveyards in the dead of night and fashioning his trophies and keepsakes from their bones and skin. And aside from Bernice he had also killed tavern owner, Mary Hogan, in 1954.

In many ways, the antics of Gein and his grisly fetishes would have been too unpalatable for the silver screen. Had producer and director Hooper featured such a macabre monster as Gein it would have had audiences fleeing for the exits as fast as Sally tries to escape Leatherface's clutches.

Gein never once used a chainsaw on his victims because that would have messed the bodies up really bad, but murders using chainsaws are not as uncommon as one might think. In 2015, in Montgomery County, the 'Quaker State' Pennsylvania, Christopher Peppelman, aged forty-eight, choked, stabbed then used a chainsaw to kill his wife, Nicole, aged forty-three. She was still alive when the buzzing began. Then he used the chainsaw to take his own life. Terminally grim, but unique, certainly.

Long-haired, out of his tiny head on drugs, Andrew Ramey Ellmaker, aged seventeen, stabbed his social worker, Teri Lea Zenner, aged twenty-six, and carved her up with a chainsaw in 2004. A Kansas judge sentenced him to fifty years without any possibility of parole. Mr Ellmaker is currently incarcerated at the maximum-security prison, Lansing CF-Central.

In 1987 Tracy Nute, then eighteen, was a troubled young man who came to Hollywood to pursue his acting dreams. He fell into sex work. After Tracy went missing his head and torso were discovered 200 miles north of the City of Angels, in a field near Madera. His arms and parts of his legs were scattered around the McBean Parkway in Valencia. At autopsy, the medical examiner determined, with not a lot of difficulty, that the body had been mutilated with a chainsaw.

When a former California State Fresno professor called Max Bernard Franc, fifty-eight, returned a hired chainsaw to a store, one would have thought that he would have had the wits to clean the blood, human bone fragments and gore out of the inner workings. After all, this is a guy who taught political science at the City University of New York, and Boston University before lecturing at Cal State, Fresno. Franc was found guilty of murder. In 1997, he died of a heart attack in prison.

In 2011 in Houston, Texas, cops discovered some human remains amongst weeds behind a house. When they searched the crawl space beneath the property, they found a trash bag containing two arms and a head. Close by was a chainsaw. Police soon arrested Noe Gerardo Morin, aged thirty-two, charging him with murder. Morin's initial protestation of innocence was rapidly dismantled when witnesses came forward to say that this was a drug-related grudge murder and Morin had actually shown a neighbour the dismembered body: 'This is what happens when someone steals from me,' he explained. For his part, the neighbour went and explained everything to the Houston PD. Mr Morin is presently housed at Eastham Unit, Lovelady, TX, and he truly is a despicable character. When one wonders where filmmakers get their ideas from, the same can be said of some real-life killers.

Co-writer Henkel also drew inspiration from a Texas murder case at the time he was writing the script and likely used it when devising the characters of the hitchhiker and the gas station owner who are instrumental in delivering Sally back to the house and Leatherface. Serial killer, Dean Corll, terrorised Houston in the earl seventies aided by two teenage accomplices, Elmer Wayne Henley and David Owen Brooks. Corll tortured, raped and murdered at least twenty-eight teenage boys and young men, many of whom were 'recruited' for him by Henley and Brooks. Henley admitted his culpability and Henkel later said that this kind of 'moral schizophrenia' was something he wanted to reflect in the characters.

The rural location of Texas plays a big part in setting the atmosphere of the movie. Here you'll find places like the small town of Rosebud in Falls County. It was here that serial killer Kenneth McDuff was born. McDuff went on to commit the infamous 'Broomstick Murders' in 1966. McDuff was driving around with an acquaintance, Roy Dale Green, allegedly 'looking for a girl' when they spotted seventeen-year-old Robert Brand, his fifteen-year-old cousin, Mark Dunman and his sixteen-year-old girlfriend, Edna Louise Sullivan. They were visiting Texas from their home in California. He used a .38 Colt revolver to threaten the trio and drove them to a field with Green following in the victims' car. There he murdered the two boys and Edna was then raped multiple times by both McDuff and Green. McDuff then asked Green for something to strangle her with. Green handed over his belt, but McDuff instead used a three-foot-long piece of broomstick that he had in his car. They then drove to a gas station to buy a Coca-Cola.

McDuff was released on parole in 1989. On 14 October 1989 the body of thirty-one-year-old Sarafia Parker was discovered. It is thought that McDuff waited just three days from his release to kill again. He was never charged with her murder but instead went back into prison on an unrelated matter. He was released again in 1990. In October 1991 McDuff murdered a sex worker, Brenda Thompson, in Waco. Brenda almost escaped when a policeman walked towards McDuff's vehicle where he had her tied up, but McDuff eluded them. Brenda's body was not discovered until 1998. Five days later McDuff was seen arguing with a seventeen-year-old sex worker, Regenia DeAnne Moore, in a Waco motel. She had been missing for seven years by the time her body was found in 1998. McDuff is also thought to have murdered Cynthia Renee Gonzalez, a twenty-three-year-old woman who went missing in 1991.

McDuff found another accomplice in Alva Hank Worley and together they murdered twenty-eight-year-old Colleen Reed after kidnapping her in plain sight of witnesses from a car wash in Austin. She was raped and tortured before she was killed. Valencia Joshua was a sex worker who was last seen alive knocking on McDuff's door in February 1992. Her body was found on a golf course nearby in March. Twenty-two-year-old Melissa Northrup was kidnapped from her job at a store. She was found in a gravel pit with her hands still tied behind her back. She was pregnant at the time. McDuff was immediately a suspect as he had worked at another branch of the store and had been seen in the vicinity.

Because McDuff's crimes were spread out across several Texas counties the investigation was difficult. McDuff was able to flee to Missouri where he lived under an assumed name until his eventual arrest in 1992. My old friend, Sheriff Larry Pamplin of Falls County, was one of the arresting officers. He had had car chases and shoot-outs with McDuff in the past. In Rosebud there isn't a road sign anywhere not adequately ventilated with bullet holes. Later, Larry got caught, then fired, for misappropriating some of the funds used for feeding his hundreds of prisoners.

On one corner, just off Main Street in Montague, Montague County, there is a cafe. It used to be a bank, and, if you care to ask the local sheriff he will proudly show you the bullet holes in the outside walls caused by Bonnie and Clyde after they made a hasty withdrawal of both other folks' money and themselves. The old hanging tree still stands in the square. The gallows are still on the top floor at the red brick courthouse, a rusty old caboose still out back. These are the sorts of places that inspire movies like *The Texas Chainsaw Massacre*. I know because I have visited all over TX; the 'Lone Star State', where all the men call their womenfolk 'ma'am', and Texas Longhorn still have the right of way.

I don't doubt that Poth is very much the same type of small town – just the right type of place for a legend about a massacre to grow. For such a seemingly insignificant place out in the sticks, per capita it has its fair share of crime. In 2019, twenty-two-year-old John Waclawczyk was found guilty of murdering his wife and a male friend with a shotgun.

But let's head back up to Plainfield, Wisconsin, hunting ground of Ed Gein. This is a village with a population fluctuating around 897 according to a 2010 census – although Plainfield's website tells us that there is a spill over into the neighbouring town of Oasis. In the winter the snow can be knee deep and as white as a chef's tall hat. This is farmstead country, where people mind their own business and expect you to mind yours – but can you do that in a place not much bigger than a couple of baseball parks?

Of course, the old Gein farmstead has long since gone but, if you take a peek at photos of any of the smallholdings of the area at the time, you will note that they all look pretty much the same – as if they are about to fall down, or as if they have been picked up by a twister, thrown fifty miles, then dropped down. Gein's place was set a long way back from the road, in a field to be precise, and it was just as overgrown as it is today now it's empty. He had nailed a sign on the gate to the property, reading: 'If you comes on here at nite you be very deader com in the morning.' He may have been something of an expert in the leather arts and crafts movement, but literary genius he was not. I have been to the site and have the T-shirt to prove it. I bought it at a local feed store. It bears the legend 'Hay, I've bin in Plainfield, an' I left,' which about sums the place up.

It was while visiting Plainfield that my TV producer and I found a bar and decided to take refreshments. It was a pool bar out on the highway. One of those places where cigarette smoke conceals the ceiling to a depth of about a foot. Let's say that it all looked as if it had been plucked out of *The Twilight Zone*. At the bar sat a gorgeous twenty-something girl dressed in a skirt, cowboy boots, and gingham shirt tied at the waist. Sitting next to her was a 35-stone heavily bearded redneck. In these sorts of joints, the locals eye newcomers with grave suspicion.

'I hear there are strange stories about the old Gein place,' I asked him.

'Yup, sure is. But you don't need to go up there at night!'

'And why is that?'

'Nobody goes up there at night cuz of the noises. Whoopin' and gruntin'. They say old Ed will come and getcha.'

'Yes, but he's dead. Right?'

'No, sir! People around here still seen him. He's still up there waiting to getcha.'

The old place might have been demolished but the ghosts of those gruesome deeds still remain.

Sometimes a killer's actions are so gruesome they inspire more than one movie. Not only did Gein inspire *The Texas Chainsaw Massacre* but he was also said to have influenced writer Robert Bloch for his 1959 novel *Psycho*, famously made into a film by Alfred Hitchcock which we will be visiting later in the book. He was also portrayed in the 1974 film *Deranged*, as well as in Rob Zombie's *House of 1000 Corpses* and *The Devil's Rejects*. Truly, his was a life and legacy of making people's skin crawl.

The Stranger Beside Me

Perhaps the best way to start this chapter is to begin with an infamous name – one that really does not need much of an introduction – Theodore 'Ted' Robert Bundy, the American sadosexual serial killer and necrophile. Indeed, when anyone thinks of a 'serial killer', invariably Bundy's name comes at the top of the list. Bundy was the reason why the term 'serial killer' came into human discourse. A charismatic and handsome man, who maintained a relationship with a young mother, Bundy lead a double life. He kidnapped, raped and murdered at least thirty young women and girls between 1974 and 1978, although it is widely thought that this number is much higher.

Ted was born Theodore Robert Cowell on 24 November 1946. He was executed in Florida's three-legged electric chair, 'Old Sparky', at the Florida State Prison, Starke, on 24 January 1989. Thereafter, he was cremated in Gainesville, Florida – a process that had already been helped along a bit when around 2000 volts at seven to twelve amps were fired through his body – with his ashes later scattered at an undisclosed location in the Cascades mountain range, Washington State.

Bundy spent part of his last night talking to a Dr James Dobson on camera. The reader can find this interview on YouTube and it makes for fascinating viewing, as it is a first-rate example of a homicidal psychopath lying through his teeth and trying to blame all of his problems, past and present, on the evils of pornography.

This interview is interesting because it also gives one a rare glimpse of someone very soon to be executed. There he is, sanctimoniously holding forth and yet shortly after he leaves the room he is given a last meal: steak, cooked medium rare, eggs-over-easy, hash browns, toast with butter and jelly, milk and juice. Then his head was shaved, a tampon was forced into his rectum and an elastic band tied around his penis before he was ordered to put on a large diaper, then redress himself – and prepare to meet his doom.

I am often asked about this pre-execution sanitary rigmarole, whether it really happens and why? This prepping for the 'hot seat' does take place and there is a very good reason for it. 'Old Sparky' didn't get this grim name for no reason. People have actually caught fire in the chair. Execution by electrocution entails forcing a lot of power through the body. It is a massive surge of power usually delivered in two jolts and can blow a man's sphincter into his trousers. The elastic band is the only easily applied means of restricting the flow of urine as the condemned usually wets himself, thus possibly shorting out the electrode attached to his shaved lower leg. The tampon is for a similar purpose. The head is shaved because, in the past, the hair has ignited, sending flames literally into the air. Nevertheless, according to rules governing the application of the death penalty in the US, this somewhat unedifying practice is linked to the constitutional prevention of cruel and unusual punishment. Yeah, right!

True crime aficionados will often find that when they watch one of the movies made about him they will note major discrepancies throughout. In fact, for anyone with a passing knowledge of Bundy's crimes, these divergences from real life will, or should, jump out at you. This is not just applicable to Bundy's history, but just about every other fiction-based-upon-fact crime movie. None of them will tell the entire truth. Perhaps it is because we aficionados of true crime are sticklers for detail. We are inclined to be pathologically precise and we will probably know more about a monster such as Bundy than even the screenplay writer, the film producer or anyone else involved in such a production.

Let's just take four of the movies to start with: *Ted Bundy* (2002) one hour and forty minutes; *The Stranger Beside Me* (2003) two hours; *Bundy: An American Icon* (2008) one hour and thirty-six minutes; *Extremely Wicked, Shocking Evil and Vile* (2019) one hour and fifty minutes.

Ted Bundy (2002) enjoyed a production budget of $1.2 million. At the time of writing it has achieved a financial return of $68, 716 – a substantial loss in my book! *The Stranger Beside Me* (2003) came from Ann Rule's excellent book of the same name, written from her first-hand experience of Bundy, and was adapted into a made-for-TV film. There are no production budget details available. However, knowing TV production companies as well I do, I can say that budgets are usually low for these projects. Nevertheless, Ann Rule knew

Bundy personally before and after his arrest, therefore, she knows her stuff. Her book is a must-read.

Perhaps the writers and producers of *Bundy: An American Icon* (2008) were using the term 'icon' in an ironic fashion. The film had an alternative tag line *Legacy of Evil* which is more appropriate for the subject matter. This has to be the trashiest serial killer biopic I have ever watched. As one reviewer wrote: 'You know these cheap true crime TV shows which have re-enactments by well-meaning amateurs who are really keen on trying to show emotion, well, the acting in those re-enactments is probably better than what we are expected to sit through in this poor excuse for a movie.' Indeed, there are so many things wrong in the movie; from the core story of poorly researched events intertwined with a lot of slow-motion flashbacks and inaccuracies, it is as if the writer and director had absolutely no regard for the facts. In fact, the production in its entirety had absolutely no regard for the grieving families and friends of Bundy's victims at all! Worst of all, it takes a terrifyingly true story and essentially makes it all rather dull and pedestrian if you ask me. Far better to watch tamer Bundy flicks such as *The Deliberate Stranger* (1986) for more interesting takes on this heinous serial killer. In this film, Mark Harmon puts in a performance that is way more accurate than not

The Riverman and the TV movie, *The Capture of the Green River Killer*, depicts Bundy assisting in the hunt for the 'Green River Killer', Gary Ridgway. But Bundy was of little real help and the movie shows that Detective Keppel was using the interviews as a way of getting Bundy to reveal more details about his own crimes.

Besides, Ridgway wasn't arrested until 30 November 2001. Bundy was executed in 1989. And again, this odd relationship between serial killer and investigator was mirrored in that of FBI Agent Clarice Starling with Hannibal Lecter. And Bundy's own modus operandi was mirrored in Buffalo Bill's. Bundy would often pretend to be injured and in need of assistance, using young women's innate good nature to lure them into a vulnerable position.

In Lars von Trier's film *The House That Jack Built* (2018), Matt Dillon plays a killer who is handsome, capable of relationships, not averse to using crutches as a prop or bludgeoning his victims to death shortly after he'd entrapped them – all the same as Bundy.

If one is so inclined, there are scores of well-researched TV documentaries and they make for very informative watching. Yet even then, they only just scratch the surface of the dreadful façade that made up one of the most God-awful serial killers who has ever lived.

In terms of reading, I highly recommend *Ted Bundy: Conversations with a Killer* by Hugh Aynesworth and Stephen G. Michaud. It is drawn from more than 150 hours of taped interviews with Bundy on death row. The book takes the reader inside the mind of one of the best-known serial killers of the last one hundred years. As for the movies – best forget them!

Monster

I am frequently asked if working with serial killers and mass murderers emotionally affects me? Generally the answer is 'No!' It is not that I have become immune to the horror, pain and immeasurable suffering these people cause to their victims – our innocent children, women and men – it is because when I am interviewing these beasts and studying them, sometimes reading thousands of documents and viewing some of the most sickening crime scene photographs, my focus is on the killer before me. When they brag and boast about their crimes I, like them, have ice running through my veins. My emotions are as cold as a windy, wintery day – but there has been one exception.

This particular case brought tears to my eyes. In fact, so upsetting was it that I took to the bottle, and everything taken together it made me quite ill. Now you don't hear that from a former Royal Marine 'Green Beret' Commando every day, do you? Indeed, at one point during this time I asked myself, 'Could this be a man/woman sentimental issue clouding my otherwise very detached thinking?' But it soon became apparent that in order to thoroughly understand Lee Wuornos and her crimes, a more sympathetic approach was called for. Indeed, as I always do when working with serial killers, I try to get right inside their heads. In Lee's case I believed I achieved just that, and this was not what I was expecting at all.

The case in question is that of Aileen Carol 'Lee' Wuornos Pralle, born Aileen Carol Pittman, 29 February 1956, and executed by lethal injection at Florida State Prison, Florida, on 9 October 2002. We shall call her 'Lee' from now on.

Lee was undoubtedly an all-American serial. She blasted seven men to their deaths with a revolver. No argument about that. She shot several of her victims many times – blew them away, with blood, brain matter and gore everywhere. When Lee drew her gun there was no messing about, no hesitation in pulling the trigger. No words came from her mouth except:

'Fuck you, motherfucker!'

BANG, BANG, BANG!

Lee was bisexual and an interstate sex worker. She did this type of work to help support herself and her lover Tyria Moore. She had been with over two hundred 'Johns', many of whom came forth after her arrest – at some risk to their own personal situation and reputation – to testify that she 'did the business and was as good as gold.' They paid her what she asked for the services they wanted, after which they both went happily on their separate ways. It was purely 'business' after all. So, I had to ask myself, what in God's name made her murder these seven particular men? Who were these 'clients'? What was it that triggered her?

These are the questions I began ruminating over as I wrote a single chapter on Lee for *Talking with Serial Killers* – first published in 2003 and still going great guns in paperback even today – for something deep in my otherwise own professional, ice-cold psyche told me that all was not as it seemed. I had to put myself inside Lee's head, and put aside for the moment all of the cop-induced and well-promoted media hysteria that was guaranteed to sell newspapers and have the world glued to their TV screens for years to come. And it was during the writing of that chapter on Lee that my tears started to flow.

They say that it is never right to speak ill of the dead. Well, my book tells the reader exactly who these seven men were. In a nutshell, some of them purported to be upstanding members of the community. One was even engaged to be married. Another was a truly violent sexual deviant who, when in drink, treated women like gutter trash. Not nice reading for their next-of-kin, to be sure, but facts are facts. Ultimately – and most certainly terminally for these seven 'clients' – was that they mistakenly thought that they could treat Lee like dirt; use her, seriously abuse her, refuse to pay then hit her. When one reads about Lee's formative years and the abuse she suffered at the hands of her grandfather, one might shed a tear, too. As a little girl, Lee went through hell and back and it is no wonder she went off the rails as a teenager to become a streetwise, troublesome renegade.

Charlize Theron is beautiful; however, when she was cast for *Monster*, she spent weeks putting on weight and her make-up was specifically designed to make her look as if life had chewed on her – or the part of the woman she was playing – real bad. And it had done. Life had gnawed at Lee's once picture-pretty looks, slim figure and at her heart and soul.

When Lee met Tyria Moore she found true love for the first time. She was devoted to Tyria. She doted on her, would do anything to please and protect her. And, if it entailed hitting the highways and byways more often on Florida's sometimes blistering hot or rain-soaked freeways to find a paying client – Lee did it without question.

Some sex workers treat their work as a business. Like any profession, if a client is satisfied with the service, he or she will return. In the main, sex work is no exception because many of these girls rely on repeat business. As the majority of her satisfied clients said, Lee had a price – nothing more and nothing less. In other words, this was 'the deal'. If people overstepped the mark and treated her like trash they would have hell to pay! Her motive for the killings was not theft, although she did steal money and personal possessions from her victims. But this was more opportunity rather than the motive behind her actions.

When Lee was arrested by the cops, Tyria turned on Lee and stitched her up. Despite this, while in custody Lee did all she could to protect Tyria's name. Smelling money, several of the police investigators also sold their 'exclusive' stories to eager newspapers, documentary-makers and film producers. I have met some of these cops and they all took back-handers. As for Moore, there was no doubt that she was present during at least one of the murders but – yep, you have guessed correctly – she got off scot-free. And Lee, her devoted lover – well, she kept her mouth shut about Tyria's involvement right to the very end.

So that brings us to the motion picture, *Monster*. The production budget was £7.15 million ($8 million) – small change as far as Hollywood budgets go when casting megastars such as Charlize Theron. At the time of writing, the film has grossed £54 million ($60.4 million), so an excellent return on that investment.

Is the movie accurate? As far as movies based on real-life crime go, it is first-rate and Theron plays the part perfectly with exceptional acting. But does the film truly outline the life and the crimes of Lee? Of course not. It is impossible to cram forty-six years of a tragic woman's life into a 106-minute cinema production. Unlike other movies about murderers, I will concede that the movie *Monster* is non-exploitative, and morally this is a very good thing.

The movie does indeed portray Lee as a victim, but do we need to be cinematically reminded of the fact that she was gang-raped by youths around the age of eleven, got pregnant, had her baby taken away from her, and was subsequently placed in a kids' shelter? That she was beaten black and blue with a leather belt while naked by her perverted stepfather, who, when not Bible-thumping, made her sleep in a shed or a car when the freezing cold winter covered everything in a thick blanket of snow? No, we do not. Therefore, as far as I am concerned, and for many valid reasons, the story of Lee Wuornos had to be painted in broad brushstrokes. There are those who will argue that the film lacks the shocking detail encompassing Lee's formative years, that her real father was a serial child sex offender who later killed himself, but with just those 106-minutes of screen time, this movie is certainly a movie to watch.

To Catch a Killer

Despite being a made-for-TV production, *To Catch a Killer* is a far more accurate true crime adaptation than anything made for the silver screen. The two-part three-hour-and-two-minute movie was made in 1992 and stars one of my favourite actors, none other than Brian Dennehy, who plays the twisted and perverted serial killer, John Wayne Gacy. Michael Riley plays Detective Lt Joseph 'Joe' Kozenczak – the latter whom I met with many others during the making of a TV documentary on Gacy.

There are many who compare *To Catch a Killer* with the 2003 horror/slasher film *Gacy*, arguing that the latter portrays the life and crimes of Gacy more thoroughly while the former seems to focus more on his life as a 'businessman' of sorts. But this misses the point because *To Catch a Killer* shows precisely how a sexual sadosexual psychopath can wear a mask of normality, businessman or not. If one is into horror/slasher films it is all about horses for courses, I guess; however, I will add this. Unlike the almost criminal pack of blatant lies which has promoted all of the Amityville films, with several of them being marketed as 'True Stories', at once exploiting the deceased, including four very young children, *To Catch a Killer* turns all of that upside down and inside out. Do we need a slasher/horror movie like *Gacy* exploiting the dead? Indeed, during the research for this chapter I re-contacted several of the law officers involved with the Des Plaines homicides. Their opinion on *Gacy* was that it was utter trash.

Unlike the Amityville films, the makers of *To Catch a Killer* were not bending the truth when they used the phrase 'based on a true story'. Within the bounds of what is acceptable to show on TV, the film does a fantastic job and the three hours duration allows the viewer to really get into the mind of Gacy and into the investigative heads of the Des Plaines Police who are hunting him. Furthermore, this movie does what it says on the tin: it broadly follows the historical narrative of the investigation leading to Gacy's arrest in December 1978. Lacking, however, is any insight into Gacy's formative years, all of which are very important in understanding how this sadosexual psychopath evolved.

As with a lot of true-life crime film treatments, some of the names have been changed for legal reasons. Many of the key witnesses and victims' family members were still alive at the time of production, as was Gacy. Furthermore, Gacy was an extremely litigious man, even on death row. Many of the killers I have met have launched lawsuits against film companies and actors. Kenneth Bianchi, one of the men responsible for the 'Hillside Strangler' murders, sued a playing card company for using his face on a pack of trading cards. This cost Bianchi almost a million bucks. Although Bianchi only received a dollar in compensation, the costs involved broke the company and destroyed the marriage and lives of the owners.

Another thing changed in *To Catch a Killer* was the name of Gacy's firm, from 'PDM Contractors', to 'LPW Construction'. PDM stood for Property Development Maintenance, a name that John's mother had suggested.

Of some amusement is the fact that, after watching the movie, Gacy wrote to Brian Dennehy accusing him of taking part in a 'fraud' film and maintaining his ridiculous claim that 'lots of people' had access to the crawl space his home where many rotting corpses were discovered. John co-owned the house along with his mother and two sisters, but he lived alone – except, of course, when he was inviting young lads in, raping, torturing and then killing them. Two men had separately lived with Gacy for short spells They were Mickel Ried and one of John's co-workers. During their investigations, police completely ruled out any of these people as having any hand in the killings, so Gacy's claim that someone else could have killed all these lads and buried them in the crawl space without his knowledge, or him noticing the stench of rotting flesh that polluted the property, was ridiculous. In fact his denial tells us more about this monster's psychopathology than much anything else.

In 1992, from his residence on death row in Menard CF, Gacy asserted his innocence, saying:

When they paint this picture that I was this monster that picked up those altar boys on the street and swatted them like flies, this is ludicrous. Whether it's Berkowitz, whether it's Bundy, whether it's Wayne Williams down

in Atlanta, or any of the others, or Charlie Manson,
I don't comment about any other cases because of the
simple fact I wasn't there. I hate it when they [the
public] put me in the same club as them.

If the people want to know the truth, or honesty of it...
that they want to be brainwashed into what they want
to believe, then, OK, fine, go ahead and kill me. But
"Vengeance is mine," sayeth the Lord, because you will
have executed someone who didn't commit the crime.

The Des Plaines Police assisted in the research and
the making of this film, which certainly does rubber
stamp law enforcement authority throughout. In fact, in
pretty much every respect, *To Catch a Killer* is faultless,
and Brian Dennehy gets as close to being John Gacy as
any actor ever could.

Over the years, I have written extensively about Mr
Gacy, the result of which the Des Plaines PD presented
me with a beautiful blue crystal mug decorated in gold –
something not every writer receives and a gift for which
I am very grateful. John Wayne Michael Gacy was born
17 March 1942. He was executed by lethal injection
on 10 May 1994, at the Stateville Correctional Center,
Crest Hill, Illinois.

Gacy had been married to women but had sexual
relationships with men too. His victims were all young
men, often teenagers. He murdered at least thirty-three
lads between 1972 and 1978, in Cook County. Most of
them met their ends in his home – a three-bedroomed,
ranch-style place at 9831 West Summerdale Avenue, Des
Plaines. You can find the address on Google Maps, but
the house, at the insistence of other residents, was quickly

demolished and where it once stood became overgrown. The land has now been purchased by a developer and, at the time of writing, a new place is being built.

To Catch a Killer certainly gives us great insight into Gacy's morally up-ended, bigoted and twisted world. I heartily recommend that the reader watch this two-part feast of true crime TV before studying his life and crimes in more depth. My book, *Talking with Serial Killers*, contains a dedicated chapter on Gacy, which you might find fascinating especially in reference to his formative years. There is some very chilling reading there too.

Gacy's life and crimes have been the subject of other dramatic treatments. The 2003 slasher, *Gacy*, also known as *The Crawl Space*, stars Mark Holton in the lead role, but the plot is as far removed from true life as is possible. It only takes a view of the official trailer to see that the story has been fabricated. It opens with Gacy's wife, Kara, played by Joleen Lutz, being woken up at 3.15 a.m. by the sound of ominous noises. Wearing a silky nightdress, she creeps around the darkened house accompanied by ominous music, eventually entering the garage where she sees a mattress, ropes and restraints. Back inside the house she starts calling out for John. Then, suddenly, there is a very loud bang and Gacy, covered in mud, pops up Jack-in-the-box-like, out of the crawl space hatch from under the house to nonchalantly say: 'Kara, I was doing something about the smell in the house.'

Anyone with even the slightest knowledge of Gacy will know that his wife hadn't slept in the same bed as him for over a decade. She looked nothing like the slim version of Kara presented on screen and, in reality, was too prim and proper to go walking around in a nightie in the middle of the night. The suggestions that the real Gacy would have enticed a young lad to the place, then raped and tortured the kid before strangling him all within a few feet of his wife is even more preposterous. And are we really to believe he would have dragged the body past the bedroom door, down into the crawl space and started digging a hole in which to bury him – at 3.15 a.m.? This is not just my opinion. The critics agreed, with Chuck Wilson, of *LA Weekly*, writing: 'The movie, *Gacy*, is unenlightening and unconvincing. It suffers from dime-store psychology and a failure to convey the subtleties of Gacy's scheming intellect.' Giving the film just half a star out of a possible five, Mike Long of *DVD Talk* said that it 'offers no suspense, no gore, and no thrills.' He concluded: 'If nothing else, a film about a serial killer should offer a glimpse inside the criminal mind. If it can't do that, it could at least be an entertaining exploitation film. *Gacy* is neither of those things and there is absolutely no reason to see this movie.' My only qualification to this particular critique would be that *no* movie based on horrific real-life events should be exploitative, period.

Before we leave John Wayne Gacy, there is a *very* short video piece, available online, called *Torment: A Gacy inspired film*. It is *very* dark, yet it truly resonated with the way I felt after interviewing this heinous serial killer on death row, for he *was* truly the stuff of our worst nightmares come true. If, after watching *Torment*, your thirst for wondering how this psychopath ticked is still not quenched, I can also recommend Popsugar's *The Killer Clown: John Wayne Gacy*, which I believe is the best short documentary on the subject.

Henry: Portrait of a Serial Killer

This may seem an odd thing to say, but Henry Lee Lucas, despite being arguably amongst the top five best – known serial killers of all time – with Bundy at the top – was easily the most boring serial killer I have ever interviewed.

I met Lucas in 1996 when he was on death row at Ellis Unit, Huntsville, Texas (death row has since been relocated to the Allan B. Polunsky Unit, in West Livingstone). Lucas had been convicted of eleven homicides and had been sentenced to death for one of those. His execution had been slated for 30 June 1976, but a stay of execution had been granted when it was revealed that details of his confession had been lifted directly from the case file to which he was given access. Henry's sentence was eventually commuted to life without parole in 1998. During the late hours of Monday, 12 March 2001, he was taken from his cell and transported to the medical area after complaining of chest pains. He was pronounced dead at 10.17 p.m. On Thursday, 15 March, he was buried at Peckerwood Hill Cemetery, the final resting place of hundreds of the Lone Star State's inmates whose bodies have been unclaimed by friends and families. Over five hundred people attended the service – more than three times the number to attend any killer's funeral in history. Beyond death, Henry Lee Lucas continues to enjoy a cult-like status amongst watchers of true crime.

At just eighty-three minutes long, *Henry: Portrait of a Serial Killer* was released in 1986. Starring Michael Rooker as Henry Lucas, and Tom Towles as Lucas's infamous partner in crime, Ottis Toole (spelt Otis in the film script). The film is almost too violent and disgusting to be endured yet received excellent reviews. This is *precisely* why the movie works for me because it doesn't cheapen death by trivialising the horror of it. Although it lacks any of the dark humour, camp in-jokes or a colourful anti-hero that so many of these films employ, it uses a mucky, slice-of-life approach to create a docu-drama that will chill anyone to the bone.

Is the film true-to-life? The answer is that it is not nor could it ever be; the very reason being that Lucas's and Toole's serial killing took place over many years – 1960 until 1983 to be precise, so, if a producer could cram twenty-three years of real-life serial killing into a one-hour-and-twenty-three-minute film then he or she deserves a place in the Magicians' Hall of Fame.

So where does *Henry: Portrait of a Serial Killer* fit in with the other movies we have looked at thus far? Actually it doesn't fit at all, for rather oddly the film seems to live in a no man's land, a bit like the drifters Mr Lucas and Mr Toole. Having met Lucas, I found the performances given by Rooker and Towles to be very true to life. That was down to first-rate casting once again. So how can I best describe Henry Lee Lucas? Based on my own interviews with him and after a careful study of his life and crimes, I suppose I could sum Lucas up in a few words: 'human pond scum' and 'a bottomfeeder'. These terms spring to mind because of Lucas's sexually perverted and twisted mind. Lucas would have sex with dogs, goats, and, at one time, he tried a live chicken. It's hard to put a number on how many people Henry and Ottis killed between 1960 and 1983. Nobody knows the full tally, not even Lucas himself. Although he was only convicted of murdering eleven people, the belief was that he'd killed even more. The single case, which earned him the death penality, was the murder of an unidentified young woman whom the cops named 'Orange Socks' simply because that was the only clothing she wore when her body was found. Her body was dumped by the side of a highway. After he was arrested Lucas went on to confess to hundreds of unsolved murders. But here justice found a fatal flaw – lying, cheating, in-it-for-themselves, smug-as-fuck, disingenuous cops.

Lucas said to me during a filmed interview: 'I done kilt nobody. Not even my own mom. My sister just done that. She will tell ya, but she's done dead, too. I know cos I kilt her too.' Shortly after Lucas found himself in cuffs, he started bullshitting in order to gain special treatment. Like so many serial killers, Henry loved publicity – the more the better. 'I kilt hundreds of people,' he boasted to anyone who leant him an ear. Word about Lucas's confessions leaked out, as it always does when a cop wants a backhander from a journalist when a serial killer is arrested – this also happened with the case of Aileen Wuornos. The media got hold of the story and descended en masse to besiege the place where Lucas was held. The press were followed by posses of detectives from all across the USA, all anxious to clear up any cold cases still chalked up on their unsolved homicide boards. In fact, the police officers in charge of the initial investigation were flooded by requests to interview Henry who, by now, had been elevated to superstar serial killer status. He had been given new dentures, new clothes and luxuries that any other prisoner would have died for. Redneck cops begged him for grip-and-grin selfies. It became a media-driven serial killer circus – one that would have been very entertaining had it not been so pathetically sick.

'The cops lied. They got lots of dead bodies, an' they ain't got what done it,' Lucas told me during an interview we filmed for the TV series, *The Serial Killers*. 'So's they takes me to where the bodies were found, tells how them people were kilt, so's I knows how I kilt them. Then I confessed to the cops and they write it down and I signed it.'

Later, a study by the Attorney General of Texas concluded Lucas had falsely confessed to a number of crimes. His sentence was then commuted to life in prison. But I wouldn't think that one would have to be an Attorney General to belatedly figure all of this out. Anyone, even someone with substandard intelligence, should have twigged on to the obvious fact that many of Henry's confessions to murder were pie-in-the-sky. In some instances he was allegedly present at three crime scenes hundreds of miles apart on the same day when he also had a proven alibi, supported by reliable witnesses. I mean you could not make this up if you tried.

It goes without saying that police knew about these discrepancies pretty much from the outset, but so keen were they to clean up their own backyards they swept it all under the carpet, thus wiping their cold case boards clean. Visit any of these US law enforcement jurisdictions today and file a public information request to see the records on any Lucas-related homicide and you'll find out that not one *single* one of them has been changed back from a Lucas kill to 'cold', and they are never likely to be either. Homicide cops never admit their mistakes – even those that have cruelly sent innocent people to their executions, and that *is* a fact, too.

Now back to the movies. *Drifter: Henry Lee Lucas* (2009). This has a one-star rating and, having watched it, I can understand why. At ninety-one minutes, it is like a guide to Lucas for beginners and that's about it.

Confessions of a Serial Killer (1985) is more extreme slasher horror than a look at real-life crimes. An eighty-nine-minute wonder *based* upon Lucas, this film was knocked up on a tiny budget. However, in saying this, it is worth a watch in any event.

If one is interested in Lucas I would start with Wikipedia to get some in-depth back history. The record here is quite accurate and lists other links too. *Henry: Portrait of a Serial Killer* is a must-watch. *Confessions of a Serial Killer* also features some revealing and subtle interactions with police that I find very true to reality.

In my book *Talking with Serial Killers* there is a lengthy chapter on Lucas, based upon hundreds of hours of visiting the crime scenes, examining police and court files, lengthy interviews with police and walking in Henry's footsteps. It gives a greater insight into his twisted mind than any movie.

Psycho

Sixty years on from its premiere, *Psycho* still ranks as one of the most iconic, mysterious, and genre-defining chillers of all time. Recognised as the first slasher movie of its kind, the deviant, sexual, criminal and psychotic content set new standards on what was acceptable in film.

Right from the off, the plot was unlike anything cinemagoers had ever seen – and atypical of director Alfred Hitchcock's usual style. Here we have a leading lady (a thirty-three-year-old Janet Leigh in top form as Phoenix secretary Marion Crane) going on the run after stealing $40,000 from her employer so she can spend the rest of her life with her hunk of a boyfriend, Sam Loomis, played by John Gavin. Using back roads to evade the police and with her progress hampered by a storm, she seeks refuge in the ramshackle Bates Motel. It is twenty minutes in before we finally meet the proprietor and main star. With no Trivago ratings to warn her about the motel's creepy host and with no other options available, Marion is grateful for the hospitality afforded to her by Anthony Perkins' strung-out, slimy but polite host, Norman Bates. He shows her to a room where she takes probably the most famous shower of all time. In a scene much copied and parodied since, Marion is naked, washing herself and at her most vulnerable when a savage killer strikes – stabbing her repeatedly in a frenzied attack.

Such a death is a particularly gory and bloody affair, not the 'clinical' result you get from shooting someone to death with a pistol, from a short distance. This is hands-on, up close and very personal. It takes a particularly cold-blooded person to stab someone, even just once, with a knife. I have met and corresponded with several female murderers who stabbed their victims multiple times until everything in close proximity becomes splashed with hot, wet, sticky blood. Imagine the horror that followed because, for them, this was not fiction. It was real. And one was even compared to the character of Norman Bates at her trial.

Joanne 'Jo' Christine Dennehy is a British woman currently serving a life sentence for the murders of three men who she stabbed to death and dumped around the county of Cambridgeshire. When I interviewed Jo at HMP Bronzefield, she was thirty-three years old – coincidentally the same age as Janet Leigh in *Psycho* – she said to me, 'Killing you, Christopher, would be good for me!' Joanne had previously told a psychiatrist that she found murder to be 'moreish' and got a taste for it after her first kill. Along with the now deceased Myra Hindley and Rose West, Dennehy is the only British female serial killer to have been handed a full natural life term. The only way she will be leaving prison will be in a pine box. I covered her story in full in my book *Love of Blood* and, in my opinion, she is the most heinous serial killer – male or female – I have ever come into contact with.

For those well-meaning experts who suggest that Dennehy's psychotic tendencies can be 'cured', I point to the fact that she had only been in prison for a night when she made threats to kill fellow murderer and inmate, Rose West. So concerned were the officers, that they placed West under 'Rule 43' protection and shipped her out to another prison in the morning. A short time later Dennehy threatened to murder another inmate she was having an affair with after learning that her lover was shortly to finish her sentence and had another woman waiting for her on the outside. That threat earned her another lengthy stretch in segregation. Joanne tried to sue the UK Home Office in the European Court of Human Rights. She was then caught having compiled a very credible 'escape kit'and sent into another period in isolation, where she then tried to cut off a prison officer's finger. From the very moment Dennehy entered prison I have warned the authorities that she will try and kill again. I believe it is only a matter of time before she does. I base this on her track record of violence.

Dennehy's crimes were brutal. Lukasz Slaboszewski, aka 'Cool Hand Luke', was her first victim. He was thirty-one when he was stabbed to death by Dennehy on Tuesday, 19 March 2013, at 11 Rolleston Garth, Dogsthorpe, Peterborough, using a small, five-inch, folding pocketknife which pierced his heart through his ribcage. Dennehy had an accomplice, Gary Stretch, and together they pushed the body into a green wheelie bin where it stayed for almost a week before being dumped into a dyke some miles away.

Ten days later, in the early hours of Good Friday at 38 Bifield, Orton Goldhay, Peterborough, Dennehy stabbed John Chapman – known affectionately as 'Uncle Albert' – multiple times. The property was a small terraced house owned by Kevin Lee – a letting agent who was married with two children. Lee had once had an affair with Dennehy. Lee wanted fifty-six-year-old Chapman evicted by any means necessary and used Dennehy and Stretch as enforcers. Dennehy, driven by her love of blood, killed him as he slept. Chapman's body also ended up in a dyke.

But if forty-eight-year-old Lee – known as 'Handsome Kev' – thought his previous relationship with Dennehy would, in some way, give him protection against her savagery he had another thing coming. On the same day Chapman met his end, Dennehy enticed Lee to 11 Rolleston Garth, which he also owned. Lee was stabbed five times in the chest whilst the maniacal Dennehy played Elvis songs and recorded the attack on her mobile phone. Then she dressed in a black sequin dress. His corpse would end up next to Slaboszewski in the dyke, his bare buttocks exposed with an aerosol forced up into his rectum.

On Tuesday, 2 April 2013, Dennehy stabbed Robin Bereza, sixty-three, twice as he walked his labrador, Samson, along Westfaling Street, Hereford at 3.35 p.m. Describing the daylight attack at her trial, he said:

I felt a blow to my right shoulder. I did not immediately realise that I was being attacked. I turned around and saw this lady. She just stared straight through me. I kicked her and made contact. It had no impact on her. She just came straight towards me and I thought she was going to mug me.

'I ran into the road. I put my hand to my jacket and saw all this blood and then it triggered and I thought, "You just want blood". She tried to come for me again. I kicked her again, but still she didn't react. I asked her, "What are you doing?" She said, "I'm hurting you. I'm going to fuckin' kill you".'

Giving more evidence against Dennehy at her trial, witness Mark Lloyd was the person to bring up the comparison with the fictional psycho, Norman Bates: 'Dennehy struck Robin Bereza like in *Psycho*, thrusting and putting her whole weight behind it. The blade of the knife was as black as the handle with blood. She stank of blood.'

Despite just two stabs, Dennehy had caused Bereza potentially fatal injuries. The deep wound to his back penetrated the chest wall, causing a haemopneumothorax (the presence of air in the pleural cavity) as well as bruising his lung and fracturing his rib. The other stab shattered his shoulder blade and fractured the bone in an upper arm. He was initially rushed to Hereford County Hospital before being airlifted to the Queen Elizabeth Hospital in Birmingham. Had the blood and air not been promptly drained from his chest through expert medical treatment, his life would have been endangered.

Just nine minutes after the unprovoked attack on Mr Bereza, Dennehy struck again. John Rogers, fifty-six, was also walking his dog, a grey lurcher, along a footpath close to the River Wye, between Golden Post and the Belmont Estate, Hunderton, Hereford, when she struck, stabbing him more than thirty times. He had deep wounds to the chest, abdomen and back and both lungs had collapsed. His bowel was perforated and exposed. So severe was the force of the wounds that nine ribs were fractured. He also received knife trauma defensive injuries to his hands and arms as he fought to defend himself.

Like Mr Bereza, he was also airlifted to Queen Elizabeth Hospital in Birmingham. He spent six hours in surgery and spent five days in the ICU, bring the total time he was in care to ten days. Again, had Rogers not received the most expert and prompt medical treatment he would have died from those injuries that day. Although he survived initially, Mr Rogers never fully recovered from his injuries. He passed away in November 2014.

Speaking at her own trial, Dennehy said: 'It was a kind of fetish. I am ashamed of the brutality and the fear that I heaped upon those two victims [Bereza and Rogers]. It was drunken cruelty, plain and simple, compelled by my lack of respect for human life. I tried to kill more times than Bonnie and Clyde. My only regret is that those two guys lived – this is no fault of my own.' The fact that all of these horrifying attacks were carried out using just a small pocketknife should show us the ferocity of a woman driven by bloodlust.

But there is nothing in Dennehy's case that would have movie audiences flocking to the cinemas. It is all too pedestrian for the silver screen. There was no intrigue, no fascinating characters, no crime of passion or double-dealing and – crucially – no mystery. Even the psychotic killer at the heart of it leaves little to the imagination. Dennehy was just drunk and evil.

Dennehy is not alone in the canon of female killers. Jodi Arias, mirroring the scene in *Psycho*, stabbed to death her all-American boyfriend, Travis Alexander, during a frenzied, homicidal rage on 4 June 2008. The onslaught started after she took photos of him in the shower. It was literally a bloodbath in every respect. There were twenty-seven stab wounds, Arias cut his throat from ear to ear and – still not satisfied – she then shot him in the head. The photographs that Arias took of her victim were what lead to her arrest and conviction.

Hitchcock filmed *Psycho* after his long-term assistant Peggy Robertson read a glowing review about Robert Bloch's novel of the same name. When a regular writer on his TV series *Alfred Hitchcock Presents* made an attempt at adapting the book, Hitchcock was less than impressed and handed it to another writer – a relative novice – Joseph Stefano to turn it into something more compelling.

Stefano made the character of Norman Bates more intriguing and complex, cutting out his fondness for alcohol and his interest in the occult and pornography. He also changed the narrative to open with Marion going on the run and built up her storyline to fill nearly half the movie. Interestingly, despite what eventually appeared on screen, the movie was considerably less gruesome than the novel. If Stefano had followed Bloch's storyline to the letter, Janet Leigh would have lost her head – literally – in the shower, not just several pints of blood.

It just goes to show that raw, unexplained violence – as demonstrated by Dennehy and Arias – does not make for a successful movie. The viewer needs to experience a deeper dive into the psychology of the monster.

It was, in fact, a real-life killer that inspired Bloch's novel in the first place. Again, loner and body-snatcher

Ed Gein – who lived just forty miles away from Bloch in Wisconsin – was the inspiration behind the fiction. So intrigued was Bloch with Gein that he decided to write a novel based on his crimes. Like Gein, Norman Bates has a deceased mother who had dominated his life. Bates keeps his house like a shrine to her memory and dresses in her clothes. Like Gein, Bates preys on women who somehow made their way to his isolated premises. It is killers like these – and the psychosis that makes them behave in a manner beyond the comprehension of most normal people – that are so compelling.

Road to Perdition

Mafia-based true-crime drama movies always put bums on seats and have done so for decades. Think, for example, of the greatest star-studded gangster film of all time – Francis Ford Coppola's 1972 masterpiece *The Godfather*. It is the most successful American film since *Gone with the Wind* (1939). Don Vito Corleone, who was played by Robert De Niro and as an old man by Marlon Brando, is thought to have been based on Carlo Gambino – a mild-mannered but ruthless Mafia leader whose career in crime lasted from the 1930s to the 1970s.

It makes good business sense to milk a great movie for all it's worth, so sequels are inevitable after a smash hit, but sadly what often follows goes downhill faster than an Olympic skier. The original film, based on Mario Puzo's bestselling novel of the same name, was – and still is – fantastic, but the follow-ups deteriorated with Al Pacino's acting becoming wooden and the plots more implausible by the minute. But what is it about this particular 'Tommy Gun' silver screen genre that draws us in?

For me *Road to Perdition* (2002) encapsulates in one hundred and seventeen minutes all that a gritty mafia-type movie should be. And, refreshingly, there was no sequel, although this was probably due to the fact that all but two of the principle characters were knocked off! The film won the Academy Award and a BAFTA for Best Cinematography and deservedly so because it perfectly captures the mood of those prohibition days when bootlegger and racketeer Alphonse Gabriel 'Al' Capone, aka 'Scarface' (1899-1947), was boss of the 'Chicago Outfit' – a step up from his early days in a certain place called Amityville.

To avoid rival mobsters and the IRS who were chasing him for tax evasion, Capone was always moving about and changing addresses. Likewise, after death he has done much the same. Following one of the biggest mob funerals ever, he started his internment in the Mount Olivet Roman Catholic Cemetery in Chicago, Illinois, where his myth continued to draw crowds. By 1952, five years after his death, there were so many tourists paying their respects that the family shifted his remains to another cemetery, leaving the headstone, engraved with the list of Capone family members' names, as a decoy. It is now believed that 'Scarface' is presently residing in section thirty-five of the Mount Carmel Catholic Cemetery, Hillside, Cook County, Illinois. But who knows for sure...

So where did director Sam Mendes and screenwriter David Self get their ideas for *Road to Perdition*? The source material was actually a comic book published by an imprint of DC. The writer, Max Collins, took inspiration from the life of gangster John Patrick Looney, of Rock

Island, Illinois who entered into a feud with Dan Drost, a once trusted henchman in his operation. Their bitter falling out led to the death of Looney's son Connor, setting Looney on a path for revenge. In the film, Mafia enforcer Mike Sullivan (played by Tom Hanks), along with his stepfather, John Rooney (Paul Newman), comes up against Rooney's son, Connor (Daniel Craig). Connor is jealous of the close bond his father shares with Mike Sullivan, who he adopted as an orphan and raised, and believes that Sullivan is a threat to his inheritance. Not only did the story draw heavily on the story of Looney and Drost but there are echoes here of *Gladiator* (2000) too, where Commodus (Joaquin Phoenix) kills his emperor father, Marcus Aurelius (Richard Harris), then sells the emperor's favourite – his adopted son Maximus (Russell Crowe) – into slavery.

In *Road to Perdition*, problems start to arise when Mike's son, Michael Jr (Tyler Hoechlin), secrets himself in a car being driven by his father to a meeting with Finn McGovern. McGovern has just buried his brother and believes the Rooney family are responsible for his death. Connor and Sullivan are under orders to just talk but the meeting ends in gunfire. Connor shoots McGovern and Sullivan has to gun down his men. Michael Jr witnesses the shootings. Driven by his own jealousy and fearing a juvenile breach of omerta, Connor decides to murder the lad along with Sullivan's wife, Annie (Jennifer Jason Leigh) and their youngest son, Peter (Liam Aiken). He succeeds only in killing Annie and the younger lad. Thereafter, Mike and his son go on the lam to escape the attentions of arch-villain and psychopathic contract killer Harlen Maguire (Jude Law).

Before the credits roll, only two characters come out of this alive – a boy and a dog. John Rooney has been shot down in a hail of Tommy gun bullets let loose by Mike Sullivan. Mike is then killed by Harlen, who in turn is shot by Mike's young son.

Some of the best gangster movies are based on true stories, like *Donnie Brasco* (1997), based on the life of FBI agent Joseph Pistone who infiltrated the Bonanno crime family. The Scorsese masterpiece *Goodfellas* (1990) was adapted from the memoirs of Henry Hill, who became an FBI informant to rat on the activities of the Lucchese family. Then there is *Scarface* (1983) whose Tony Montana was inspired by Al Capone. And *Carlito's Way* (1993) adapted from the novels by Edwin Torres, a criminal defence attorney who used his own experience of growing up in gang-riddled New York in the late 1940s and early 1950s as food for his fiction.

On the surface, the classic mobster movie seems little more than a glorification of violence, drug abuse and immorality. However, the greatest crime films cut to the heart of the desire for the American Dream. Mobsters from the Italian mafia to the Japanese Yakuza turn to crime as a means of independence and fulfilling dreams of financial success. And of course, looking for validation in the criminal underworld often leads to bloodshed and sorrow.

Another classic of the genre is Quentin Tarantino's signature postmodern epic *Pulp Fiction* (1994). The depth of the overall plot to this film is astounding. One minute dark and moody, the next riddled with black comedy and unforgettable lines that have made their way into popular culture and parlance.

A personal favourite film of mine is *The Untouchables* (1987), starring Kevin Costner as Federal prohibition agent Eliot Ness and Sean Connery as Irish American bureau officer Jim Malone. Malone sums up the risks their work involves when he says to Ness: 'You just fulfilled the first rule of law enforcement: make sure when your shift is over you go home alive. Here endeth the lesson.' With Robert De Niro almost unrecognisable as Al Capone and the late Billy Drago bringing Frank Nitti back to life, it's an all-star cast. There's a wealth of source material concerning Eliot Ness's famous attempts to put Al Capone behind bars and director Brian De Palma lit a rocket under the subject, elevating the tale from a standard cat and mouse chase to an emotionally complex epic.

I remember that, as a youngster, I sat with eyes glued to the American TV series *The Untouchables* (1959-1963), starring Robert Stack as Eliot Ness and narrated by Walter Winchell. And in this series, we again find much professional cinematic integrity and attention to detail. During the 1930s, Winchell was a close friend of Owney Madden, New York's number one gang leader of the prohibition era. Word got to Winchell that he was about to be 'hit' so he fled to California, returning to New York having had an epiphany and with a new enthusiasm for 'G-Men' or government men. He befriended John Edgar Hoover, the first Director of the Federal Bureau of Investigation, and Winchell was solely responsible for turning Louis 'Lepke' Bachalter of 'Murder Inc' over to the FBI chief – the rat!

Sadly for us Brits, we don't have a real-life Eliot Ness in our mob-world DNA. What we do have is *Get Carter*

(1971) starring Michael Cain as the ruthless, remorseless and stubborn London gangster, Jack Carter, who goes after the man who has killed his brother. Ian Hendry, George Sewell, Alun Armstrong and Britt Ekland all turn the movie into one of the best hard-boiled crime dramas made in the UK. The icing on the cake is that all of the characters are totally believable, too.

Lock, Stock and Two Smoking Barrels (1998), *The Krays* (1990) and *McVicar* (1980) are other British-made crime movies that do exactly what they promise to do on the tin. As gritty as sand and gravel mix; an aggregate of real-life true-crime events carefully selected and combined with fiction to provide a cinematic product that stays in our memories for decades to come. They are as British as the Union Flag, or as British as London's Blind Beggar pub in Whitechapel, where, on 10 March 1966, Ronnie Kray shot dead a Richardson gang member, the mouthy George Cornell, while he was sitting at the bar.

I interviewed the now deceased Ronnie Kray years ago while he was in Broadmoor Hospital, Crowthorne, Berkshire. He was wearing a dark, bespoke suit, black, polished shoes, his shirt cuffs ironed to a crease and sporting a huge diamond and gold 'RK' signet ring. Ron snapped his fingers at an officer, barking, 'Hey, you! Get this gentleman a Coke and don't hang about.'

'Yes, Ronnie. Straightaway sir!' came the reply.

I liked that very much indeed.

For me, any movie starring Jason Statham has to be a must-watch. However, throw in Vinnie Jones and Leonard 'Lenny' McLean, Sting and Patrick H. 'P.H.' Moriarty, who plays 'Harry the Hatchet', and you get an energetic, clever crime movie that looks into various little pockets of underworld life – sex, gambling, drugs and hired thug – all salted with black comedy. I am of course talking about *Snatch* (2000). Best of all in this stellar cast is perhaps the late Dennis Farina as Avi and Alan Ford as Brick Top. The plot is based on bare-knuckle boxing and gambling. It punches the viewer in the face as hard as any Tyson right-hander too.

And as for Al Capone? His life story was a natural source of inspiration for the cinema. It's a story that has been told many times since Paul Muni played Camonte in *Scarface* (1932) – most notably in Roger Corman's *St Valentine's Day Massacre* in 1967. There were rumours that Capone was offered $2 million at the beginning of the 1930s to play himself in the film but he never actually went to Hollywood.

I loved the 1970s ITV series *The Sweeney*: a fifty-three-part drama focusing on two members of the Metropolitan Police's Flying Squad. It starred the late John Thaw as Detective Inspector Jack Regan, and Dennis Waterman as his partner, Detective Sergeant George Carter. The 2012 movie of the same name starring Ray Winstone and Ben Drew works to a point, but as in all of these take-offs, us true-crime buffs will always remember the original versions, and this is why the repeats are constantly shown on the box.

Incidentally, the character of Jack Regan was based on Detective Inspector Jack Slipper, aka 'Slipper of the Yard', who was known for his unconventional approach. Slipper was amongst those responsible for bringing to justice the killers of PC Geoffrey Roger Fox (aged forty-one), Detective Constable David Stanley Wombwell (aged twenty-six) and Detective Sergeant Christopher

Tippett Head (aged thirty). These officers were shot and murdered by Harry Maurice Roberts and John Witney in Braybrook Street, near Wormwood Scrubs, London, on Friday, 12 August 1966.

For me, nobody has done more for the image of the British police than the actor Jack Warner OBE (1895-1981). Warner became a familiar and beloved figure to the public as friendly Sergeant Dixon in the BBC series *Dixon of Dock Green*. For almost two decades, I was glued to the TV when Warner opened each programme with his characteristic rocking on the heels of his shoes and 'Evenin' all' – a greeting which has come to be associated with the police force to this very day. Warner first appeared in the role in the 1950 feature film, *The Blue Lamp*, which ends with Dixon's death at the hands of the villain, played by none other than Dirk Bogarde. So effective was Warner in his portrayal, that audiences found the sad ending unbearable. The British public's refusal to accept the untimely death of Dixon was also testimony to public regard for the police in those days. After the film company received thousands of complaints, it was decided to resurrect Dixon for his very own TV series. So, if you happen to be passing by the East London Cemetery and Crematorium, Newham, Greater London, you might wish to place some flowers on Warner's grave, then stand back and say: 'Evenin' all'. Jack would like this very much indeed.

Seven

In 1995 the David Fincher-directed neo-noir thriller *Seven* (stylised as *Se7en*) hit cinema screens. The box office receipts for the film stand at $327.3 million worldwide, all coming from a $30 million production budget. To put this into some form of financial perspective, James Cameron's *Titanic* (1997) was the most expensive film ever made at the time, with a production budget of $200 million it has since received $2.187 *billion* in receipts.

Nevertheless, *Seven* won several awards including the MTV Movie Award for Movie of the Year, MTV Movie Award for Best Villain (Kevin Spacey), London Critics' Circle Award Actor of the Year (Morgan Freeman), and the MTV Movie Award for Most Desirable Male (Brad Pitt). The film was nominated for Best Film Editing at the 68th Academy Awards but lost to *Apollo 13*.

Before the film hit our screens in 1995 few people could probably name every sin. David Fincher's disturbing crime thriller made us all think of the weaknesses of the human condition in a new light and forced us to consider the eternal battles fought out between sins and virtues. The seven deadly sins are: gluttony, greed, sloth, lust, pride, envy and wrath. How did these concepts find their way into the imaginations of writer, Andrew Kevin Walker, and director, David Fincher, when they produced *Seven*? What echoes of real life can we find in this film?

There are movies too numerous to mention where a retired or a retiring cop is called upon to crack one last case, and *Seven* uses this device. Police detective William Somerset (Morgan Freeman) takes on his final homicide case with the aid of newly transferred rookie detective David Mills (Brad Pitt). As they are called upon to investigate a number of elaborate and shockingly sick murders, they soon realise that they are dealing with a serial killer.

Our serial killer in *Seven* is John Doe, played by Kevin Spacey. The names 'John Doe' for males, and 'Jane Doe' for females, are multiple-use names that are used when the true name of a person is unknown or is being intentionally concealed. *Seven* is set in America so, in the context of US law enforcement, such names are often used to refer to a corpse whose identity is unknown or unconfirmed. A visit to any mortuary will almost always reveal a big toe tag with 'Jane Doe 1' written on it. The names are also often used to refer to a hypothetical 'everyman' in other contexts. This becomes interesting when referenced to the character of John Doe in *Seven*.

Seven, like *The Silence of the Lambs*, is a compilation of true crime, real-life events all rolled into a cinematic feast of horror. John Doe kills his first victim, played by Bob Mack, by forcing him to eat too much and then kicking him hard in the stomach till he dies. The dead man's head is then forced down into a bowl of food. Gruesome stuff. Although I cannot find a single case where a person has been murdered in this manner, I can see where this idea *may* have come from. For there are cases where people have, in fact, died from eating too much food – the sin of gluttony. A handful of reports over the years document accounts of people who literally ate themselves to death, or at least came dangerously close to busting a gut. Japanese doctors wrote in a 2003 case report that a forty-nine-year-old man's 'excessive over-eating' caused his stomach to burst, killing him. An earlier 1991 case report describes a similar 'spontaneous rupture' in an adult's stomach 'after overindulgence in food and drink.' And of course – and I may be wrong here – the kicking into the stomach of a person who has seriously overeaten would certainly rupture the gut and hasten death.

The murder representing 'sloth' sees the unknown killer tying his victim up on a bed for almost a year. In keeping him alive for the better part of this time, but not allowing him to move freely, 'John Doe' is telling us how laziness affects a person. Fortunately, as hard as I have tried, I cannot find a real-life murder case where some poor soul has been imprisoned this way. Indeed, the scenario is fantastical. Perhaps I have missed something here because the human body surely needs food and water to survive. In *Seven*, this would have entailed John Doe popping in every few days carrying victuals. The sloth crime is, like the previous gluttony invention, a flight of fantasy with the very not-so-subtle warning that physical inactivity increases the risk of many major adverse health problems.

I very much like the 'greed' murder scene, for here the cops arrive and find a defence attorney bound and kneeling on the floor of his office. Next to his corpse is a pound of his flesh weighed on a scale. Detectives Somerset and Mills suspect that the lawyer was given a knife and instructed to cut the flesh from his own body. 'Greed' is written in blood on the floor. A note is found, saying: 'One pound of flesh, no more no less, no cartilage, no bone, but only flesh.' This phrase comes from the character Shylock, a moneylender, in the play *The Merchant of Venice* (c. 1596) by William Shakespeare. The etymology of 'Shylock' is of being an 'usurer, merciless creditor'.

But there is, in the 'greed' murder in *Seven*, some real-life grounding for it. It is not an unusual event in the US for an aggrieved person to blow their attorney's or their bank manager's head off with a 12-gauge shotgun over some disagreement or other, thus exacting one's pound of flesh.

Pride? Ah, yes, this is the case where the victim has her nose sliced off by 'John Doe'. The two detectives find a bottle of tranquillisers glued to the palm of one hand, a mobile phone to the other. There is nothing unique in the latter because almost everyone living in the western hemisphere has a mobile phone glued to one hand or the other these days, nights and weekends. I've seen diners first chop up their food so they can dispose of a knife and use only the fork to feed uninterrupted while they gabble away on their phone. Soon, in the better classes of restaurants, they will get the waiter to do it all for them – feeding them as well as serving them. This victim chooses suicide rather than calling for help because of her pride in her former beauty. Although there is some evidence to be found in the saying 'Beauty is Never Tarnished', disfigured women will most like commit suicide, especially if the damage is really severe. Although I believe that millionairess Jocelyn Wildenstein, aka 'Catwoman', is still modifying her bizarre facial appearance to this very day, I'd put money on it that when the sun starts to rise in the morning she truly wishes she could reset her face to its factory settings – proving that money cannot buy everything.

Once again, I cannot find a single, even similar, murder case in the grim annals of murder history. The motives for the 'lust' and 'envy' segments of *Seven* leave me in the dark. However, I do get the 'wrath' that drives the final scene when Detective Mills learns that his wife has been decapitated and he shoots her killer, 'John Doe', in the head. Wouldn't you? For 'John Doe' is the greatest sinner of them all. At least our MTV Movie Award winner for Most Desirable Male (Brad Pitt) gets his pound of flesh.

Somewhat unusually for Hollywood, what we have here is not a compendium of real-life murder, but a selection of Biblically alleged sins that can hasten one's demise. Furthermore, where we do find crime fiction turning real-life on its head is that in real-life there has never been a case where a lone killer has used so many *different ways* of committing serial murder. No one has been that calculating. But this is the silver screen where anything and *everything* can happen. This is what puts bums on seats … watching other people suffer with heroes stepping up to the plate.

As with Harris for *The Silence of the Lambs,* screenwriter Walker drew on various killers, came up with imaginative ways to die and used the Bible as his starting point, much like I have done here. Having varying types of murder and vastly different MOs all committed by one man is about as far from homicidal reality as it is possible to get.

INTERMISSION –
What puts bums on seats?

It is at this point in the proceedings I would like to take a short break. We can call it an 'intermission' – one where the reader may, if needs be, take time out while allowing me to make a few observations.

Thus far we have seen how Dr Hannibal Lecter metamorphosed from an innocuous, real-life surgeon who killed his lover in a pique of jealousy into a character who has sustained a multi-million-dollar movie franchise. This is all down to the amazing imagination of Thomas Harris, a brilliant writer who knows his real-life criminology subject extremely well. Harris picked and mixed different crime stories and psychopathologies but although the resulting movies were terrifying they were not cinematic exploitations of real-life dead people. At the end of the day, the Hannibal Lecter movies are simply scary and very entertaining because this is what Thomas Harris and his screenplay writers intended them to be.

In contrast are the morbid exploitations of real-life mass-murder: *The Amityville Horror* and all of the sequels. It is like pissing over the graves of the dead and, as you might have noticed, this upsets me deeply. I sometimes wonder whether any of these filmmakers would have been so quick to exploit the suffering of others had they lost a loved one under such terrible circumstances and viewed the broken body in a morgue.

And, come to that, see what my old friend Judge Stuart Namm thought about lead cops, Detective Dennis Rafferty and Lt Robert Dunn, whom appeared in a New York investigation into the Suffolk County Homicide Division, detailing police malpractice at the most gross level.

The end scene in *Seven* – where Detective Mills shoots John Doe for killing his wife, Tracy – is a masterstroke of how *we would all* feel if someone had murdered a loved one. Up until the conclusion, the film's plot resonates in a Biblical and over-imaginative way. Just like Hannibal Lecter, we all know that a killer such as John Doe could never exist in the real world, so we view the storyline from a distance. The horror does not affect us because we know that it is a million miles from reality. We have no personal connection to the victims. Actually we have no real connection with the killer either because for most of the time he is hidden from us – and the cops too. However, we *do* get to know rookie homicide detective David Mills.

The trope of rookie cop and father-figure mentor can be somewhat 'old hat', as it is often used in fictional crime movies. But it really works in *Seven*. This is why casting the right actors for the right movie is so important – in the case of *Seven*, this is fictional crime writing and cinematic psychology at its best. We feel the heartache now befallen Detective Mills and we see

Somerset pleading with his partner not to ruin his own life in avenging the life of his wife. But Mills does shoot John Doe. Wouldn't *you* do the same given half the chance? I know I would.

The Stranger Beside Me movie and *The Amityville Horror* is a case in point, with the exception being that Ann Rule's book of the same name is, quite literally, based on fact. Thereafter, as so often with sequels, each subsequent film goes drastically downhill as the box office receipts prove. But still these trash movies are being churned out; simply rehashing and rehashing and piling bullshit upon bullshit till the end of time, I guess.

I can see no other way of saying this, but it *is* cinematic exploitation of the most dreadful serial-killer spree in US history. And these producers of films about Bundy are imaginative with their titles too, always sticking the name 'Bundy' someplace on the poster and thus guaranteeing that people are drawn to buy a ticket like wasps are to jam.

With this being said, there are a few excellent Bundy Land TV documentaries on the internet worth a watch if you are hooked on Ted. Nevertheless, there is a greater value here – an intrinsic value to other filmmakers: Bundy's MO, of course.

I have written extensively and in more detail about the numerous ways, means and methods serial killers use to lure their prey to their doom. Perhaps the most infamous one is 'The Mystery Man in a Sling'. On several occasions Bundy, with his arm in a sling, deliberately dropped the books he was carrying when a young co-ed approached him. He chose the locations carefully, usually during the twilight hours, and he asked them to help him carry them to his vehicle parked nearby. What young woman would not want to help a peer in distress? These girls were never seen alive again. On another occasion Bundy brazenly struck in broad daylight. It was Sunday, 14 July 1974. The location was Lake Sammamish State Park, Washington State, where the internationally known beer maker, Rainier, was holding its annual picnic. The edges of the lake were packed with hundreds of young people, soaking up drink and the sun.

With his arm in a sling, Bundy convinced Janice Ott to go with him on the premise of helping with his sailboat. Hours after Janice disappeared, Denise Naslund was also persuaded to help the man in the sling. Both were probably killed that same day. It took two months for their bodies to be found on the hillsides near Issaquah.

I stand to be corrected, but in my experience of dealing with and interviewing serial killers, Harvey 'The Hammer' Louis Carignan stands out as a homicidal sex maniac. Carignan, like Bundy, vented his hatred upon women because, deep down, he hated females with a passion. It is the bludgeoning and slow strangulation that gives killers like Bundy and Carignan their perverse sexual 'pleasure'. They revel in treating their victims like garbage. As Michael Bruce Ross, aka 'The Roadside Strangler', admitted to me when I interviewed him on death row, Somers Prison, Connecticut: 'Yes. I used them, abused them then dumped them [the bodies] like so much trash.'

Bundy used his extensive knowledge of law enforcement methodologies to elude identification and capture for years, all of which made him an unusual mix of an 'organised' *and* 'disorganised' killer. Serial killers are usually one or the other. For example, Bundy never used a firearm due to the noise they made and the ballistic evidence they left behind – something that Butch DeFeo was unconcerned with when he committed the Amityville homicides using his Marlin rifle. Bundy used blunt instruments to bludgeon and he also strangled his victims to death – two relatively quiet methods of killing.

Bundy also liked to use aliases. One was 'Officer Roseland' which he used to entice Carol DaRonch to get into his 'unmarked police car'. Carol escaped Bundy and testified against him in court. It is a sad state of affairs but there have been cases where police officers have abused their uniform and badge to exploit, coerce, rape and even murder women. Called the 'shield' in the US and in the UK a 'warrant card' – both are symbols of the ultimate authority, and it *is* a given that one *has* to yield to this authority, most especially young people... most especially those who are raised to respect the law.

The 'Officer Roseland' fake cop ploy used by Bundy is not unique by a long chalk and there are scores of cases easily found on the internet. Some of these criminals I have interviewed or corresponded with so I will briefly highlight a few of them here.

David Alan Gore was a redneck serial killer who was executed by lethal injection on 12 April 2012. A former deputy sheriff, he confessed to six murders of very young women in Vero Beach and Indian River County, Florida, in the 1980s. During his appeal process, he was foolish enough to write lengthy letters to me detailing his horrendous crimes. He told me how he used his cop badge and sometimes his police cruiser to abduct his victims. He would then strip them naked, hang them up in his barn, then rape and torture them – even slicing off their skin while they were still alive. I passed on Gore's letters to the prosecutors and subsequently his execution was fast-tracked.

The letters and documents Gore sent to me proved, at least to my mind, that it *was* Gore who committed the killings. He and his half-cousin, Fred Waterfield, had been dubbed by the media as the 'Killing Cousins' although Gore had, several times, retracted his initial claims that Waterfield had been involved. He had written to the cops via his attorney and had other signed witness affidavits to this effect. But Waterfield remained in the picture.

I wrote to Fred Waterfield and his attorney. I was then supplied with over a hundred documents and affidavits from witnesses, several of whom alleged that they had coerced by police to make false statements. These were later withdrawn, but all of this was swept under the carpet. Indeed there was evidence that it was Fred Waterfield who happened on Gore about to kill a girl. Waterfield intervened and saved her life. She testified to police that Waterfield had plucked her from a terrible death, but the police ignored this too.

Despite this and all of the literature to be found online, Fred Waterfield is now serving two consecutive life sentences for two of the murders. Not everything published about Waterfield online is factual. Apart from myself, and Waterfield and his attorney, no one else had seen the material that was sent to me. I copied most of the important documents and posted them by secure mail to the DA. I didn't even receive the courtesy of a reply.

Kenneth Bianchi and Angelo 'Tony' Buono were dubbed by the media, 'The Hillside Stranglers'. I have extensively written about this killing tag team, and a chapter in my book *Talking with Serial Killers* covers their case in some depth. I corresponded with Bianchi for many years and interviewed him at Washington State Penitentiary, Walla Walla, Washington State. I also made a TV documentary about the Hillside murders.

During their Los Angeles serial killing spree, these two gutless low-lives posed as undercover cops as they cruised around LA seeking victims. They had bought fake police shields at a swap meet and used them to 'arrest' several sex workers, and eventually two little schoolgirls, Dolores Ann 'Dolly' Cepeda, aged twelve, and Sonja Marie Johnson, aged fourteen. The girls were 'arrested' on the suspicion of shoplifting in the Eagle Plaza shopping mall. All of the victims were taken to Buono's home in Glendale, where they suffered the most terrible torture and rape ordeals that anyone can imagine before they were murdered.

Along with lead cop, LAPD Homicide Detective Leroy Orozco, I visited the dumping site where Dolly and Sonja had been disposed of naked and legs spread apart. It was on Landau and Stadium Way, a hillside overlooking a flood canal and the city in a hazy distance. It was a place known for illegal dumping of trash and a sign next to the girls' bodies read: 'DO NOT DUMP YOUR TRASH HERE!'

Bianchi also worked alone using a similar ruse. On one occasion he knocked on the door of a girl he wanted to date. He told her that he was now a cop. He flashed his phoney shield and told her that her car parked outside had been broken into. She was never seen alive again.

On 12 January 1979, Bianchi was arrested in Bellingham, Washington State. He had become the prime suspect in the murders of two co-eds, Diane A. Wilder, aged twenty-seven, and Karen L. Mandic, aged twenty-two. Employed as a menial security patrol officer for the Whatcom Security Agency (WSA), Bianchi had told Karen that he was 'Captain Bianchi'. He had offered the girls a well-paid, cash-in-hand house-sitting job. Bianchi had keys to the property. As soon as they arrived he raped and strangled them to death. He heaved the bodies onto the back seat of Karen's car and parked it in a cul-de-sac a short distance away.

Gerard John Schaefer: This evil bastard was actually assassinated, suffering multiple stabs to the body, on 3 December 1995, while awaiting execution on death row, Florida State Prison, Starke. With two confirmed kills, but possibly guilty of more than thirty, he was dubbed by the media 'The Killer Cop'. Schaefer was a sheriff's deputy in Martin County, Florida. His murder was possibly a 'hit'. At the time, he was attempting to sue one of America's most famous FBI offender profilers and the cost of defending this extremely spurious action would have ruined this agent's life and career. But this is merely very well informed, blue chip 'speculation', if you catch my drift? In any event you simply cannot piss off the FBI – it would be a bit like upsetting a dead

Indian chief or even a live one, because the shit is bound to hit the proverbial fan!

So there we have it. Bundy's fake policeman guise and his arm in a sling pretext has provided grist for many a film producer's mill, copycat killings and research material for hundreds of fictional crime writers ever since. His ploy evoked sympathy from his intended prey, who would have been feeling sorry for him, his misfortune, situation and circumstances.

The Green Mile

The Green Mile (1999) is a prison drama adapted from a novel by Stephen King. It features an unusual inmate who displays inexplicable healing powers and has a profound effect on the people around him, bringing light into a place of death and suffering. How real could such a story compare to what life is really like on death row? 'The Green Mile' refers to the block in the fictional Cold Mountain Louisiana Penitentiary, which houses the prisoners on death row and is so called because of the colour of the linoleum floor. During my several decades as a criminologist I have walked many a so-called 'green mile'. I have met many men who will soon hear the call 'Dead man walking' as they make their way on their final journey. However, I have not encountered any inmates like John Coffey, the mysterious central character of *The Green Mile*.

King set his story during the Great Depression and the film's director Frank Darabont (who also helmed another classic prison move adaptation of a King novel, *The Shawshank Redemption*) gives us a fictional cinematic feast with memorable characters, humour, outrage and emotional release on a Dickensian scale. Most of the film was shot in a real prison, the former Tennessee Penitentiary, Cockrill Bend Boulevard, in West Nashville. Closed in 1992, the penitentiary previously featured in Bruce Beresford's *Last Dance* (1996) with Sharon Stone, and also Tom Mangold's *Walk the Line* (2005) with Joaquin Phoenix as Johnny Cash. The result demonstrates why locations are so important in conveying atmosphere.

The film sets reminded me of Washington State Penitentiary (WSP), Walla Walla, Washington State. During one of my visits there I paid special attention to this facility's 'correctional' history. WSP – known as 'The Concrete Mamma' or the 'Mother of all Prisons' – opened in 1886 when executions were carried out by hanging. Today, aside from their final meal, the condemned are offered a more varied menu: hanging or lethal injection. Those were the days of hard labour, when a prison stretch really did mean 'hard time'. Convicts were chain-ganged into road building and forestry work. They wore standard leg irons, often called 'Ringquist Boots' which weighed seven pounds or just over three kilograms. The basils, or rings, were fitted around a convict's ankles and then hot riveted by a blacksmith to prevent removal. The irons chafed the ankles red-raw and made work difficult and tiring in what was called 'The Convict Shuffle'. They also made loud clinking noises with every movement – hence the term 'in the clink'.

Back then, WSP's death row was very much like 'the row' portrayed in *The Green Mile*. On one side of the block were the holding cells with the tier leading to the death chamber or 'the execution shed', where the gallows were situated. In more recent years the lethal injection gurney was also close by, but it was by then called an 'execution suite'.

Sing Sing Prison in Ossining, New York, had an electric chair in situ, but it was relocated to the Green Haven Correctional Facility, Stormville, New York State. It's all very antiquated and never used these days, but still they have the steel headpiece with the dried sponge inside it. I know because I have sat in it – with the power off, of course, and much to the chagrin of my TV producer, Frazer Ashford, who might have liked to flick the switch as payback for all the headaches I caused him!

The sponge was crucial in the act of execution. Watching Eduard Delacroix die in 'Old Sparky' in one of *The Green Mile*'s most disturbing scenes is as close as it can be to reality when there is a 'technical glitch' – as people who are in the electric chair sales and refurbishment business call it. In *The Green Mile*, the devious little worm of a prison guard, Officer Percy Wetmore (Doug Hutchison), deliberately doesn't wet the sea sponge that is applied to Eduard's head. A wet sponge would have enabled the current to pass straight through the head and out through the leg electrode to earth – giving a very positive result for the department of corrections and a shockingly negative result for the person who at that very moment would dearly wish that he was someplace else. Note the subtle 'Wetmore' and 'wet the sponge'. This is an example of a cleverly casted name worked into a plot, one probably missed by millions of viewers. It is such imaginative creations that create first-rate movies.

Until quite recently, an almost identical oak electric chair was situated at the Somers Prison, Connecticut, where I interviewed the serial killer Michael Bruce Ross. This chair, with deep scratch marks at the ends of the arms, had not been used since the execution of Joseph 'Mad Dog' Taborsky, on 17 May 1960. Taborsky had carried out a string of armed robberies and murders – beating, shooting and pistol whipping his victims – and had earned the moniker with his savagery. Since then the chair had fallen into such a state of disrepair it would have cost tens of thousands of dollars to make it serviceable. The Department of Corrections would have to find an electrician who knew how to wire it up and then train a new generation of prison officers on how to use it properly so that the condemned was not blown through the roof when the power was switched on. Instead they moved Death Row to the nearby, more modern Osborn Correctional Institution, and installed a suite for lethal injections which are more hygienic surgical affairs with tubes and shiny stainless-steel trolleys and men wearing white coats. These days it's all about making the killing of a person seem humane, with an eye on budgets, of course.

I got to know Michael Ross very well and, due to my relationship with him, he admitted to guilt in two cold case homicides: that of Dzung Ngoc Tu, aged twenty-five and killed on 12 May 1981, and Paula Perrera, aged sixteen and murdered in March 1982. Ross also admitted to a number of other very serious post-mortem sex offences. At the age of forty-five, Ross was executed by lethal injection on 13 May 2005. For his last meal, he ate turkey a la king, rice, mixed vegetables, white bread, fruit and a beverage. In the execution suite, after the chemicals entered his body, he coughed once as his lungs collapsed, his face turned ashen and the hair on his neck started to rise – which is common during the last phase of dying. He was pronounced dead at 2.25 a.m. He is buried at the Benedictine Grange Cemetery, Redding, Connecticut.

I was proud to receive letters of commendation from the two law enforcement agencies concerned and my dealings with Ross are covered in more detail in my book *Talking with Serial Killers*. The transcripts of those confessions, some made on camera and others confirmed to police, are now with DCI Martin Brunning of Bedfordshire, Cambridgeshire and Hertfordshire Major Crime Unit, who also assisted me in the research for my book *Love of Blood* about Joanne Dennehy.

In *The Green Mile,* the character 'Wild Bill' uses course language, makes explicit sexual references, causes trouble, covers his cell in excrement, annoys the guards, intimidates Officer Percy Wetmore and racially insults John Coffey. But he gets his nickname not because of his behaviour but because he lectures the guards about the difference between the historical American soldier, 'Wild Bill Hickok', and 'Billy the Kid'.

I have visited many death rows where most of the time the condemned give absolutely no trouble at all. Appellate processes aside, they know that they are 'Dead Men Walking' and live with it. Occasionally they do have a little spat, yet every inmate does, no matter what security category he is subject to. There are tiers in most US Super Max facilities that house the extremely psychotic, cruel, cunning, odious and dangerous. A walk through any of these places is like visiting Bedlam. The inmates screech and behave just like 'Wild Bill' does, and this why there is a yellow line on the floor that separates the cell and the far wall. Cross the line, get too close to the bars, and the prisoners *will* spit and *will* throw urine and faeces all over you. Sam Rockwell played the part in a manner as close as one can get to a real-life homicidal psychopath: one totally devoid of altruistic qualities and with a total disregard towards women – not only had he raped and killed two little girls but one of the three people he killed during a robbery was pregnant. In many ways the fictional 'Wild Bill' reminds me of one of the most evil of all American serial killers – Donald Henry Gaskins Jr. Born 31 March 1933, and executed in South Carolina's electric chair on 6 September 1991, Gaskins was convicted of nine homicides, although he claimed one hundred and ten kills – a figure which is highly unlikely.

Dubbed by the media 'Pee Wee', 'the meanest man in America', 'the redneck Charles Manson', 'Junior Parrott' and 'The Hitchhiker Killer', Gaskin's crime spree is something the reader might wish to look up after a meal, *not* beforehand. Indeed, if you can find a copy on the internet, I thoroughly recommend *Final Truth: The Autobiography of a Mass Murderer/Serial Killer* by Donald Henry Gaskins and Wilton Earle.

The plot of *The Green Mile* is pure fantasy, which makes it more perennial as far as prison motion pictures go. It is cinematically iconic, in my opinion, setting the benchmark for any death row movie. But what makes these 'good movies' so special is the amount of in-depth research that goes into the writing and production.

They set a 'gold standard', whereas too many others feel thrown together with a blood-curdling title as though that's enough.

Other excellent films that accurately convey prison life are *Birdman of Alcatraz* (1962) starring Burt Lancaster, Telly Savalas, Karl Malden, Thelma Ritter and Leonard Penn; *Escape from Alcatraz* (1979) starring Clint Eastwood, Patrick McGoohan and Danny Glover; *Papillion* (1973) featuring Steve McQueen, Dustin Hoffman and Woodrow Parfrey.

I have visited Alcatraz, or 'The Rock', but desisted from travelling to the penal colony of Bagne de Cayenne otherwise known as 'Devil's Island' in French Guiana, where Henri Charriere – 'Papillon' – eventually ended up because of the prevalence of mosquitoes and tropical diseases there. Some of these movies were more-or-less based on real-life case histories and were thoroughly researched. However, *Papillon*, the 1969 bestselling memoir penned by Charriere (1906-1973), wasn't a completely true account of his time on Devil's Island. Charriere claimed that the prison had a terribly harsh regime, full of brutality and inhumane treatment. In fact, historians later found that most of his account had been embellished and much of his story had been acquired from the experiences of others. This was later changed when a remake of *Papillon* was released in 2017, with Louis Dega being played by Rami Malek. The facility on Devil's Island still provides inspiration for writers to this very day.

The film *Scum* (1979) is also worth mentioning, a brutal, slap-in-the-face film. *Scum* is the story of two boys' struggle for survival in Borstal, a notorious British reformatory. The film was based on an original 1977 script which was supposed to be screened as part of BBC's *Play for Today* series. It was not shown until 1991, having been banned by the BBC for fourteen years. In the meantime, the film version was filmed and released. In *Scum,* we have Carlin played by Ray Winstone, Archer played by Mick Ford, a diamond performance from Philip Jackson playing Officer Greaves, and P.H. Moriarty as Hunt. Borstal inmate Carlin rapidly becomes the new 'Daddy' – the alpha among the inmates who controls a wing – on the block. He keeps the other inmates in check, dealing out punishment according to the prisoners' code – all of which makes the officers' lives easier and leads to greater privileges for 'Daddy'.

This is a common situation in many correctional institutions. *Scum* portrays a juvenile version of the hierarchies that exist in adult prison regimes, where 'Daddy' characters also thrive. These hierarchies are not found so much on death rows and in segregated housing units (SHUs) – where the inmates are held under much higher security conditions and allowed far less freedom of movement – but they are rife in the general prison populations, especially in America's 'dog-eat-dog' correctional system. Here, the 'Daddy' characters are called 'Shot Callers' for obvious reasons. They have obtained this rank through their gangster status, use of brute force, unrelenting intimidation, or sheer power of personality. Like Carlin in *Scum*, they earn the respect and loyalty of other cons and, in turn, they gain a measure of deference from the prison officers. Much like the Mafia, with a 'Capo', or 'Caporegime', the 'Shot Caller' will be similar in status to the captain or lieutenant of a division. He heads a crew of soldier-style convicts and reports directly to a boss who hands down the instructions. While in prison, Al Capone still called the shots. So did the mobster and criminal mastermind Charles 'Lucky' Luciano (1897-1962), who established the first 'Commission' or governing body of US Mafia. Like Luciano and Capone, the 'Shot Caller' may well be a member of an organised crime group like the 'Bloods', the 'Crips', the 'Black Mafia', the 'Yardies' or the 'Aryan Nations'. He is answerable to his boss on the outside, who will, if needs be, order the killing of a 'snitch', or that some other form of punitive punishment is dished out inside prison.

Behind bars, the 'Shot Caller' is king. He has his own crew who follow his orders without question – their messages, or 'kites', are often written in cypher form and exchanged between inmates, often on nothing more than a small piece of yellow paper, maybe four inches square. Like the notes that junior high school kids pass during classes, these are often written upon both sides and usually folded many times until they are the size of a penny, making them easy to pass furtively.

Every general prison population in the world has its 'Shot Callers'. We even see this in the British TV comedy series *Porridge,* with Harry Grout (Peter Vaughan) and his strongman, Crusher (John Dair). Sadly, so many of these loveable actors have long gone now, but they will remain with us because many of us still invite them around for their repeats, on the box, at Christmas. *Porridge* was all about humour, which of course real prison life is not. It would be wrong to suggest there aren't many moments of light-heartedness behind the steel gates though. I recall one funny exchange with a security officer at HMP Winchester, who quipped to a new intake of screws: 'Read my lips, all of you. In here there are a lot of thieves so don't trust any of them. If I see someone riding a motorcycle around one of the wings, what question do I ask myself? Well, I am going to be asking myself: "Where did he get the petrol?".'

Even on death row there is a hierarchy of sorts, with child murderers at the bottom and cop killers at the top. This I discovered when I was given time with Washington State Penitentiary's death row inmates. Before walking WSP's 'green mile', I talked at length to an assistant warden, who gave me the heads-up on each of the men I would be talking to. There was one inmate who they said commanded the respect of his peers. I requested that the officers stay way back as I walked the yellow line, before asking this particular inmate if I could approach his cell – or his 'house'. He agreed and I came up to the bars. For a few moments I explained who I was, that I had come all the way from the UK, and why I was at the pen. The psychology behind my approach was simple. He knew his position as the alpha on the row. Now a man who had the power to ask the guards to stand back was addressing him. It would have fostered mutual trust and, maybe, some mutual respect. I asked, if it was OK with him, if he and his fellow cons could join me out on the tier for a chat, soft drinks and some candy. Within minutes – unlock – and I had these condemned men sitting around me on that tier. So even here there is a pecking order and always one con who holds sway. Of course, after eating a prison diet for twelve years, who would not want to leap at the chance of a bar of candy and an ice-cold fizzy drink? But the fact that the nod came from the top dog helped smooth the process and respected the order of things in the block.

North American prisons are extremely tough places in which to survive, especially when you consider each fresh-faced newbie first shuffles from a prison bus imagining that hell on earth awaits him. Recognising the natural order and finding your place within it goes some way to making the stretch a little less painful.

The Shawshank Redemption

The Shawshank Redemption (1994) is another classic film now firmly implanted in our cinematic history. Based on another of Stephen King's bestselling books, the story finds Andy Dufresne, played by Tim Robbins, framed for killing his wife and her lover and sentenced to two consecutive life sentences in prison. The filming location was a real prison – the Ohio State Reformatory, 100 Reformatory Road, in Mansfield. Built between 1889 and 1910, this facility remained operational until 1990 when it was closed via a federal court order. Much of the original building has now been demolished but the East Cell Block remains the largest free-standing cell block in the world. The building now hosts a museum that helps fund rehabilitation projects.

On the surface, *The Shawshank Redemption* appears to be just another in a long line of get-out-of-jail-free movies, but there is a lot more going on than this. It is actually a snapshot of the problems within the US judicial and penal system which existed not only at that time but have endured until today. In the film we have a totally corrupt, Bible-thumping bigot of a prison warden, Samuel Norton, portrayed admirably by Bob Gunton, and equally evil senior prison officer, Heywood (William Sadler). Our band of convicts are Ellis Boyd 'Red' Redding (Morgan Freeman), Brooks Hatlen (James Whitmore), and Skeet (Larry Brandenburg). This makes a superb cast. The film also has about the best philosophical one-liner, when Red says: 'Get busy living, or get busy dying.'

The movie is now so well loved it's easy to forget that it was slow to take off. Premiering at the Toronto Film Festival in September 1994, it garnered good reviews but business was slow. Its original gross takings of £16 million ($18 million) didn't even cover its production costs. Renowned US film critic Roger Ebert recalls: 'It took in only $10 million after winning seven Oscar nominations, including best picture. Then it hit the home video market. By April 1999, it was occupying first place in the Internet Movie Database (IMDb) worldwide vote of the 250 best films.'

This feel-good prison-break movie reminds me so much of the crooked, devious US cops, judges, attorneys and corrupt correctional officers with whom I have come into contact throughout my career. Of course, the majority of prison officials are a credit to their institutions, but you can still find many real-life examples of Samuel Norton and Officer Heywood. There are crooked attorneys and judges in just about every single US state.

Innocent people and prisoners with learning disabilities or mental health issues are still being executed in America. Often the cops, district attorneys and judges suspect these people are innocent, but they still sign off their orders for lethal injection, deliver them to 'Old Sparky' or lock them away on full life tariffs. You just have to take a look at the amazing work carried out by Clive Stafford Smith, a British attorney and anti-death penalty campaigner who specialises in civil rights, to see how many injustices there are within the penal system. Stafford Smith has represented more than a hundred detainees from Guantanamo Bay since 2002.

A miscarriage of justice that echoed the plight of *The Shawshank Redemption*'s Andy Dufrense was that of Joseph Roger O'Dell III, who I got to know very well over the years of his incarceration for a murder he claims he did not commit. When tragic Helen Schartner was savagely beaten, raped and murdered outside a bar in Virginia Beach on 5 February 1985, he was wrongly accused of the atrocity. O'Dell, who had already been convicted of murder, always declared his innocence, admitting that he had done 'many terrible things' in his life but not this crime. The police messed about with his DNA and blood and concocted a story to cover up the claims made by David Mark Pruett that he was the real killer. Although O'Dell was not Italian and had no connection with Italy, his case was taken up by the Italian government which abhors capital punishment and he was also championed by the Pope and Mother Theresa. Despite all that support – and the fact he was completely innocent – he was still executed by lethal injection at 9.16 p.m. on 24 July 1997.

It is also claimed on the internet and elsewhere that the US Supreme Court rejected his last-minute appeal. This is incorrect, too. His appeal papers arrived on time, but a clerk failed to open them, and, with a deadline looming, this was a deliberate attempt to push his appeal out-of-time – which it did. Effectively and officially, his appeal arrived too late. The cops were bent, as were the prosecutors, who dismissed claims that police officers would fabricate evidence, saying it was 'unheard of.'

Pruett, who confessed to Schartner's murder, was himself executed by electrocution on 16 December 1993 for committing two rapes, robbery and multiple stabbing homicides. His victims were Kentucky Fried Chicken co-worker Debra McInnis, and Pruett's own best friend, Wilma Harvey, at Virginia Beach, in 1997 and 1998. He gave a detailed account of how he murdered Schartner, but this all went by the wayside. The entire case has become a terrible stain on the US judicial system.

When such gross injustices occur, it's important that movies such as *The Shawshank Redemption* exist to serve a non-exploitative moral purpose. They offer up subliminal messages for, although fictional, many of these movie plots are based upon real-life cases, people and circumstances – they are simply made a little more enjoyable for our consumption, for if we were to see the real stories behind the silver screen it is likely we would feel physically sick.

Cool Hand Luke

There's no denying *Cool Hand Luke* (1967) has some real meat on its bones. Starring Paul Newman in the lead role as Luke Jackson, George Kennedy stars as Dragline, the prison leader or 'Daddy' character I was describing in the last chapter. Strother Martin plays the Captain, the warden of the prison who has it in for Luke. The supporting cast includes Harry Dean Stanton and Dennis Hopper. It's an entirely believable, must-watch crime drama based on those 'good ole' days' when chain gangs were part and parcel of the American punishment system.

Set in the fifties, Jackson is a small-time criminal and is arrested for cutting parking meters in Florida. He is sentenced to a brace of years in what is euphemistically called a 'prison farm'. Handsome and rebellious, he sets out to make the sadistic, baccy-chewing Captain and his staff's duties a misery. Despite several stints in the much-hated confinement box, Jackson becomes a hero amongst his fellow cons as well as a pain in the ass for those guarding them. As film critic Pat Brosnan wrote: 'Incredible movie. Best ever made. This atmospheric film oozes class. From the grasshoppers chirping to the beads of sweat running down the inmates' faces, everything brings you into their world. You are there with them. The acting is sublime ... besides Newman's powerful prescience, George Kennedy stole the show with an amazing delivery as the top dog in the prison with his slow change of mind towards Luke and his madness towards authority. If you love watching movies, watch this one on your own, lights down and volume up, you will be transported back in time.'

The reason the movie is so convincing is down to the source material. Writer of the original novel the film is based on, Donn Pearce, was a former safebreaker and counterfeiter so drew on his own experiences on the chain gang while serving time in a Florida jail. He penned the script along with Frank Pierson, who would go on to win an Academy Award for *Dog Day Afternoon*, the Al Pacino movie based on an actual bank robbery.

For *Cool Hand Luke*, director Stuart Rosenberg created a sublime prison drama with pitch perfect cinematography, screenplay settings, score and acting. The entire cast delivered superlative performances, with Newman portraying one of the most notable rebels ever to hit the silver screen.

But what were these prison farms like in the real world? We all know that inmates were historically set to work to earn part of their keep as part of the prison system. In England, in Victorian times, breaking rocks, sewing mailbags and 'pickin' oakum' out of ship's rope was, indeed, punishment with a capital 'P'. In fact, every prison establishment around the world today has work programmes of one sort or another for its inmates: the inmates can earn credits and extra perks for doing this work, too.

For example, think of *Porridge*, with Fletcher getting a job as the librarian in Slade Prison. Some inmates get to work in the kitchen, or chop wood, or if it is a prison farm, the mechanically minded are given the task of servicing and repairing vehicles and tractors. I spent a week at the Washington State Penitentiary where I interviewed sadosexual serial killer and one of the men behind the infamous Hillside Strangler murders, Kenneth Bianchi, and other stone-cold killers. Here they have the 'License Tag Shop' where all of the vehicle number plates for the State of Washington are stamped out. And, believe it or not the serial killer, Arthur Shawcross, repaired locks during his incarceration at the Sullivan Correctional Facility. The now executed British serial killer, John Martin Scripps, was taught butchery skills while in prison on the Isle of Wight, where he was serving a fifteen-year sentence for drug smuggling. He served just three years of this sentence before he escaped (walked out of the gate) from an open prison. Scripps took his butchery skills with him to Singapore and Thailand. In both countries he killed and dismembered three people as if he were disjointing carcasses. South African tourist Gerard George Lowe was murdered in Singapore by Scripps. And then Sheila Mae Damude and her son, Darin, met their end at his hands in Phuket. It's also thought that some years before this – and before he'd learned the butchery trade – Scripps had killed backpacker Timothy McDowell in Cancun and fed him to alligators.

So, what has happened to the 'good ole' days' of breaking up rocks in a quarry as they used to do at

Dartmoor Prison in bleak, grey Princetown, out on the desolate and boggy Devon moors? The problem these days is that anything considered hard work in a prison is a fundamental breach of the inmates' human rights. Some would argue that it's only since the removal of hard labour that a culture exists where a little, mindless thug who is in prison for almost beating a granny to death, is up on the roof having been denied his TV privileges with a lot more like-minded cretins ripping off the slates, behaving like monkeys in a zoo and pissing over everyone who is trying to put out the fire they have just started.

I am all up for the 'three strikes and out' punishment doctrine in some US states. Three convictions and one is locked up forever and a day, even if the last offence is merely stealing a tube of toothpaste. The problem in the UK these days is that prisons are made so comfortable that many of the inmates are anxious to return. Just before Christmas each year it's not uncommon for the courts to see an increase in down-and-outs heaving bricks through off-licence windows or some similar premises. Off they go to prison where a warm bed awaits; Christmas dinner with all of the trimmings; a medical check and treatment 'as required'; dentistry; a new set of civvies and a nice handful of cash plus a travel pass to wherever they want to go upon their release.

Reformation, indeed – so I cannot see a reason why the UK authorities cannot build a prison on an island way, way off the north coast of Scotland – say, for example, off Cape Wrath, the most north-westerly point, which is lashed by storms every five minutes.

Make it someplace a long, long way away for visitors to get to and call it the Scottish equivalent of Alcatraz – meaning 'Island of Pelicans' in the US Indian dialect, but we could use 'Island of Puffins', instead. The only prisons on any UK islands are Parkhurst and Albany on the sunshine-bathed Isle of Wight; a short hovercraft trip from Southsea, free bus tickets thrown in, and an extra allowance for the missus to bring the kids and smuggle in as much dope as she can.

On my 1986 visit to Ellis Unit, in Walker County, Texas, where I interviewed serial killers Henry Lee Lucas and Kenneth Allen McDuff, I recall driving towards the facility seeing the grey-brown dust rising from the roads and fields where the prisoners and hoe squads laboured away under a scorching sun. It is a prison farm in every respect, situated twelve miles north of the death house at the Walls Prison, Huntsville. Although officially banned back then, the inmates were working, dressed in coveralls with 'CONVICT' on the back, shackled by leg irons, in groups of five men linked by eight-foot chains, eight hours a day, trudging along the shimmering bitumen highway collecting trash. *This* is punishment. When one inmate suddenly stops and jerks the chain, it cuts into his ankle and the legs of those with him. Simply going from A to B requires all five to cooperate. Teenager, Christopher Jabba Coachman, then serving twenty years for attempted murder, says: 'People who drive past the chain gang may think twice about committing a crime. It might teach people a lesson.'

His views echo the philosophy of former Sheriff of Maricopa County, Arizona, Joseph 'Joe' Michael Arpaio, who made his prisoners wear pink suits, housed them in a tent city and made them shuffle around town looking like the criminals they actually were. Although he has come unstuck these days, Joe's history can be found on Wikipedia and his depositions found on YouTube. They make for a fascinating insight as to what a hardline sheriff should be – loyal to his men and as hard as a blacksmith's nails.

One can also read an informative article online about Prison Plantations – The Marshall Project, so one can then see just how accurate *Cool Hand Luke* is. It is a fascinating subject indeed. What struck me more than anything when visiting the Ellis Unit were the guards carrying rifles. Riding tall in their saddles, Ray Bans on, packing heat, wearing silvery spurs and sweat-stained grimy Stetsons. One of them told me that should a man make a break for it he could shoot his eyes out at three-hundred yards. Now that's a deterrent!

Deliverance

'Deliverance' is the state of being saved from a painful, bad or dangerous experience. This was not what was on offer to several of the characters of the 1972 movie, *Deliverance*. It is one hour and fifty minutes of intense, disturbing, unsettling and psychologically dark viewing.

You can almost imagine the producer setting the scene for the cast – Burt Reynolds as macho Lewis Medlock, Jon Voight as his sparring partner Ed Gentry, Ned Beatty as the 'pretty mouthed' Bobby Trippe and Ronny Cox as the hapless Drew Ballinger.

Producer: 'Now guys, here is what we are up to. Leave the families at home next weekend because here's the plot, OK? We're going to take you to one of most desolate locations along the Chattooga River, deep into the wilderness of the Tallulah Gorge in the "Peach State" – where everything that is gonna happen to you won't be peachy at all. Upon your arrival, you will be given two canoes, after which you will be pushed off into the current and left to get on with it.

'En route to your travel destination at "Aintry", some umpteen miles downriver, ya'll will be stopping off at one of the historic, tourist hillbilly sites where you will meet some of the locals and be serenaded by Billy Redden, playing Lonnie. You, Ronny, will be strumming away as Drew in a banjo contest. But we all hope Drew has made a will because before long he's going to drown.

'Burt, you'll be playing Lewis, who will suffer a compound fracture of a leg.

'Ned, you'll be playing Bobby, so you are gonna get stripped naked then sodomised by a toothless, inbred backwoodsman. Jon, your character, Ed, barely escapes the same thanks to Drew – who has some previous experience in outdoor camping trips in his RV – who turns up to kill Toothless played by Herbert 'Cowboy' Coward but allows his pal, Bill Denison McKinney, to escape back to his still to work on some more "Moonshine".

'Well guys, that's the general plot. Mind how ya'll go now, and ya'll have a nice day now, ya'll hear!'

Based upon a James Dickey novel, John Boorman's survival movie has a beautiful visual style that balances the film's message of machismo. It's a haunting masterpiece that exhumes our most primal fears and is as deep and dark as the landscape where it was filmed.

For as long as man has been able to hold a spear, hunting has been programmed into the survival parts of our DNA; primarily for survival and territorial reasons and as a source of rich food. It has warped in some minds into something darker, such as a taste for stalking, serial homicide and even cannibalism.

So, really I think that the Georgia hillbillies got a bit of a bad rap in *Deliverance*, although it is fair to say that I have never heard of these sorts of goings-on happening in the New Forest near to where I live, or anywhere along the Thames as far as I can tell. A real-life stalker killer is echoed in the scenes we see in *Deliverance*, although he was not a direct influence on the plot or film. He was in fact killing from a year before the film's release in 1971 and he didn't stop until he was caught in 1983: Robert 'Bob' Christian Hansen.

Hansen abducted and murdered at least seventeen women – many just teenagers – around Anchorage, Alaska. Hansen would stalk and hunt his victims down in the icy wilderness with his Ruger Mini-14 and a buck knife.

Hansen had a face that only a mother could love, one look at his mugshot tells you quite a lot about this stuttering, acne-scarred, cowardly serial killer. His first marriage ended almost before the couple had warmed up their bed. Perhaps because Hansen had a penchant for committing arson, assault, kidnapping, weapons offences, theft, and was socially inclined to commit insurance fraud, rape and murder? He must have been quite the catch for the two women who agreed to marry him, even raise families with him.

If I were to be a borderline Christian soul, I would give him some credit for having had a bit of a rough start in life. Hansen was a weak child – skinny and painfully shy. He was afflicted with a stutter and severe acne that left him permanently scarred – but so are thousands of other youngsters but they don't go out hunting humans to rape and then kill them. Hansen was also diagnosed as bipolar with schizophrenic episodes, and a psychiatrist said that he had an 'infantile personality'. Shunned by most of the girls at school, it was said that

Hansen grew up hating women and nursing fantasies of cruel revenge. Hansen blamed all of his sins on his dad: a Danish immigrant and a baker by trade. Christian Hansen was allegedly a domineering father and taught his son to practice hunting with a bow and arrow. His wayward son 'found refuge in these pastimes'.

The FBI arrested Hansen in 1983 and he was handed a somewhat optimistic 461-year prison sentence after being found guilty of murder. He never quite made it to the end of his sentence. He passed away at the Alaska Regional Hospital on 21 August 2014, aged seventy-five. The cause of death was down to 'undisclosed, lingering health conditions'. The Butcher Baker's goose was finally cooked!

Snowtown

With a population of around 470, the small town of Snowtown, on the main road and rail link between Adelaide and Perth in South Australia, and a small, disused bank vault would seem to be the most unlikely of places to store the remains of eight bodies in drums full of acid.

But the grisly discovery on 20 May 1999 would put Snowtown on the crime map – joining places like Amityville as towns forever associated with evil acts of violence and creating such a lasting stigma that the town's inhabitants even considered changing its name.

'The Snowtown murders' or the 'bodies in barrels murders' as they came to be known, were a series of twelve killings committed between August 1992 and May 1999. Only one victim was actually killed in Snowtown itself, with the others murdered in and around Adelaide. The killers were John Justin Bunting, Robert Joe Wagner and James 'Jamie' Spyridon Vlassakis. Their trial became the longest and most publicised in Australian history, leading to a short-term boost in curious tourists that eventually plagued the town.

When the body of twenty-two-year-old Clinton Trezise was found at the Lower Light township in 1994, South Australian Police had no idea it was part of anything bigger and no connection was established initially to Bunting. When Thomas Trevilyan, aged eighteen, died in 1997 cops initially thought it was suicide. It was only when Elizabeth Haydon disappeared in 1998 that the trail led police to Snowtown where, in six plastic barrels in the disused bank vault, they found the remains of Elizabeth and seven more victims. These were: Michael 'Michelle' Gardiner, aged nineteen, who'd been killed in September 1997; Barry 'Vanessa' Lane, Wagner's forty-two year old ex-partner, killed in October 1997; Gavin Porter, Vlassakis's twenty-nine-year-old friend, killed in April 1998; Troy Youde, Vlassakis's twenty-one-year-old half-brother, killed in August 1998; Frederick Brooks, aged eighteen, killed in September 1998; Gary O'Dwyer, aged twenty-nine, killed in October 1998; Elizabeth Haydon, Mark Haydon's wife and Frederick Brooks's aunt, aged thirty-seven, killed 21 November 1998, and David Johnson, Vlassakis's twenty-four-year-old stepbrother, killed 9 May 1999.

Suzanne Allen, Bunting's ex-girlfriend, was forty-seven when she died in November 1996. Her body was found on 23 May 1999 and she was considered a likely victim of the killers, although they were never convicted of her murder. Ray Davies was aged twenty-six and living in a caravan in Allen's back garden when he was killed in December 1995. His body was found on 26 May 1999, and this was also linked to the killers. Their bodies were found buried in the backyard of Bunting's house in Adelaide, where Vlassakis also lived.

Cops believed the victims in the barrels had been killed elsewhere and held in several locations in South Australia before being moved to Snowtown that year, possibly because the killers feared they were under investigation. Police charged Bunting, Wagner, Vlassakis and Mark Haydon the day after finding the bodies.

Although a motive was never properly established, one witness, Ms Raelene Brown, whose boyfriend was friends with Bunting, said that he was always talking about killing and torture. On the occasions that she saw Bunting and Haydon together at her home, she heard them talk about 'weird things'. Bunting spoke in detail about paedophiles, homosexuals and torturing and killing people, as well as making people disappear.

One theory is that Bunting was a sort of leader and persuaded Wagner, Vlassakis and Haydon. Bunting was the one who directed the action and then helped his pals to dispose of the bodies as a kind of sub-undertaker. Bunting had been sexually abused by a friend of his older brother when he was eight years old and he was known to have a strong hatred of homosexuals or anyone he thought might be a paedophile. Perhaps he thought if the victims were paedophiles, homosexuals or generally weak it made them, in his eyes, not fit to live.

Another theory was that the killings had a robbery motive. In several cases the victims were tortured in order to obtain their identities, social security payments and details of their bank accounts.

John Bunting was convicted of eleven murders and Robert Wagner of ten, only three of which he confessed to. Haydon was convicted on five counts of assisting with the murders. He admitted to two. Vlassakis pleaded guilty to four murders and provided testimony in exchange for a lesser sentence. As the established ringleader, Bunting is now considered Australia's worst ever serial killer.

Bunting's chosen method of body disposal was somewhat gruesomely reminiscent of that used by John Edward 'J. R.' Robinson, aka 'The Slavemaster', who I spent much time corresponding with and which I wrote about in my book *Talking with Serial Killers*. He was found guilty in 2003 of three murders committed in the Kansas City area and received the death sentence for two of them.

Robinson, aka Bonner, aka Thomas, aka Turner, has been on death row (Special Management) at the El Dorado Correctional Facility in Kansas since his conviction in 2002. The similarities between the cases are striking. Perhaps if Bunting and Robinson had heard of each other's cases before their killing spree they might have evaded justice for longer – or decided not to dump their bodies in barrels, as this is how both were caught.

Much like Plainfield, Wisconsin, Snowtown is a remote location. Australia might be the world's sixth largest country by total landmass, but the country's population density is 2.8 inhabitants per square kilometre, making it the lowest in the world. This means that one could walk hundreds of miles in any direction and never meet another person. Compare this with England with 426 people per square kilometre, or Macau, with 20,400 people per square kilometre, and you get an idea of how vast Australia is. Curiously, Macau has a far lower per capita homicide rate than Australia, so it's not always a given that living on top of one another leads to violence.

In fact, the Aussie outback is notorious for the tragedies that befall its travellers. The bodies of a young couple, both nineteen years of age, were discovered along with their three-year-old child on 7 November 2018, in the Northern Territory. The body of a twelve-year-old boy believed to be a family friend was found a day later 120 metres from the other three corpses. The group had set off from Willowra on 2 November and were headed towards Jarra when their car broke down on a journey which should have taken roughly five hours. The car had suffered a flat tyre and had run out of fuel. In a region when it might be months before you see another vehicle it's easy to perish without proper supplies.

And so, with all this available outback to choose from to bury bodies, why did Bunting, Wagner and Vlassakis choose to dispose of many of the corpses in a disused bank vault, in a town the size of a baseball pitch? Burying two other bodies in Bunting's backyard also proves these killers weren't the sharpest tools in the box. Given how crucial the disposal of bodies is to evading justice, you would think serial killers would give it serious consideration. A number of them I have interviewed were arrested simply because they did not consider how nor where to dispose of their deceased prey afterwards. They earn the accolade 'serial killer' due to the fact that they have murdered three or more times with a cooling off period in between the events. If one doesn't quite hit the three mark then one is then called an 'emerging serial killer' – a loser to be sure. So, the general idea is to stay free of handcuffs and leg iron restraints for as long as one possibly can. Which is why I am surprised Bunting and his accomplices didn't recognise that burying a person's body under the floorboards of your own home was more risky than, say, digging a deep hole some 800 kilometres away, in which you can throw the deceased, set it ablaze and cover with a lot of dirt before scooting off. Although Bunting and his gang stayed out of chains for seven years, had they not disposed of the bodies where they did they might have gone on to enjoy murdering and robbing innocent Aussies until they retired.

Another lesson a sensible serial killer quickly learns is to keep the victim's body in one's possession for as short a time as is possible, alleviating the risk of being stopped by a traffic cop who finds a corpse in the trunk of your motor. Joel Rifkin, aka 'Joel the Ripper', who murdered nine women (possibly a lot more) in New York City, and on Long Island, between 1989 and 1993, slipped up here when a New York State cop spotted him driving his Mazda pickup without a rear licence plate on the Southern State Parkway. Failing to yield to the signal to pull over, a high-speed chase ensued. It ended with Rifkin losing control and crashing into a utility pole directly in front of the courthouse where he later stood trial. Talk about prescient! In the back of the Mazda troopers discovered the decomposing body of his final victim, sex worker and dancer, twenty-two-year-old Tiffany Bresciani. Tiffany also happened to be the girlfriend of Dave Rubinstein, aka 'Dave Insurgent', of the punk rock band 'Reagan Youth'.

In 1994, Rifkin was sentenced to 203 years to life. At the time of writing he is sixty-one years old, so it is unlikely he will see out his custodial tariff. He is now incarcerated at the Clinton Correctional Facility,

Clinton County, upstate New York, where he makes vehicle licence plates. If that isn't an unrelenting Groundhog Day life sentence, I don't know what is.

Snowtown (2011), the movie adaptation of the killings, was a critical success, winning the AATC Awards for Best Lead Actor (Daniel Henshall), Best Supporting Actress (Louise Harris), Award for Best Direction (Justin Kurzel), and Best Adapted Screenplay (Shaun Grant). As true-crime-based motion pictures go it's a powerful dramatisation and at times it is almost too much to watch. It is disturbing, unsettling, gruesome and thought-provoking all at once. Critic Peter Bradshaw said of the film: 'Here is a docu-Jacobean nightmare, and a dysfunctional stepfamily drama, based on the career of Australia's most notorious serial killer.'

Helter Skelter

Charles Manson needs little introduction. The flower-power-era petty thief became infamous as a 'cult leader' in the sixties when he formed the 'Manson Family' – a quasi-commune consisting of dope heads, social security spongers and posh city gals. Manson's hold over his followers was so powerful that he convinced them to kill for him. The family were responsible for nine horrific murders at four different locations in the summer of 1969.

Manson didn't quite match up to a proper cult, such as the Branch Davidians. Led by David Koresh, and quartered at Mount Carmel Centre Ranch, Axtell, Texas, at least the Branch Davidians had a permanent home while the Manson Family more-or-less squatted in and around the Spahn Movie Ranch, near Chatsworth, and the Barker Ranch in Panamint Valley, aka 'Death Valley'. Although Koresh and his cult were stockpiling illegal weapons, they had not murdered anyone or posed the slightest threat to human life before the FBI, US Marshals Service, ATF and local law enforcement moved in, all of which resulted in a catastrophic firefight.

The entire place burned to the ground, four agents were killed, sixteen wounded, with a total of seventy-six wiped out on 19 April 1993. If there ever was one hysterically over-reactive law enforcement cock-up, this had to be it.

When it comes to cults, 'The Peoples Temple Agricultural Project', aka 'Jonestown', led by the oily, overweight Reverend Jim Jones, was the real deal. Jones convinced his followers to commit mass suicide by drinking cyanide-laced drinks. This resulted in 918 of them dying at a nearby airstrip in Port Kaituma, and a temple-run building in Georgetown, the capital city of Guyana, on 18 November 1978.

So, when we learn that Manson's desert-dwelling cult consisted of approximately one hundred mostly part-time followers, who were always out of their tiny minds on hallucinogenic drugs, one wonders how Charlie ever earned the title of 'cult leader' in the first place? It is true that some of the followers of his 'teachings' were teenagers and young women from middle-class backgrounds, who became radicalised by his verbal bullshit. Manson managed to convince them into thinking that the hippie culture and out-in-the-sticks communal living and getting pregnant at the drop of a hat was due to the Word of the Lord manifesting in himself. How they fell for it beggars belief. Yet many of these girls did just that and the dreadful result was real-life human butchery – killing on a scale that shocks us even today.

Helter Skelter (1976) was a two-part made-for-TV drama that aired in the US over two nights. It was based on the 1974 book, *Helter Skelter: The True Story of the Manson Murders*, written by prosecutor, Vincent T. Bugliosi Jr and Curt Gentry. In other countries it was screened in cinemas, and included additional footage including nudity, foul language and even more violence than the original TV showing. We have to remember that, in the seventies, naked bodies didn't exist on the box – at least not in the USA.

Bugliosi prosecuted 105 out of 106 felony jury trials during his career and secured twenty-one murder convictions. However, he is best known as being the Los Angeles District Attorney who prosecuted Charles Manson and the other defendants accused of the seven Tate-LaBianca murders committed on 9 and 10 August 1969. Bugliosi passed away in June 2015, aged eighty. Curtis Marsena 'Curt' Gentry was an American writer who won the Edgar Award for Best Fact Crime, he died in San Francisco, aged eighty-three, on 10 July 2014. *Helter Skelter*'s screenplay was written by James 'Pappy' Pinckney Miller – his penname being 'JP'. So the film *Helter Skelter* had some serious credentials behind it.

Although it could be argued that Charles Manson never actually murdered anyone, he did at least incite some of his followers to kill by proxy. The first attempted homicide was that of Bernard 'Lotsapoppa' Crowe, in Hollywood, on 1 July 1969. The weapon used was a .22-calibre Hi-Standard Buntline revolver. The perpetrator was Manson himself and he botched the job. I mean, how can anyone botch-up killing someone by firing a revolver at point-blank range into their head?

The Gary Allen Hinman murder took place at 964 Old Topanga Canyon Road, Topanga, California, around 25 to 27 July 1969. Cause of death was shooting and stabbing. The perpetrators were Bobby Beausoleil, Susan Atkins, Mary Brunner and Charles Manson.

However, it is the night of 8 August 1969 that saw the slaughter of Sharon Tate, Jay Sebring, Abigail Folger, Voytek Frykowski and Steven Parent, that will remain embedded into our true-crime-to-cinema DNA for ever.

The murders and butchery that took place at 10050 Cielo Drive, Los Angeles, have been well documented, not in the least by Bugliosi and Gentry's bestselling book. Sharon Tate, the wife of director Roman Polanski, was eight months pregnant, and both she and her unborn child were killed. Her friends Jay Sebring, hairstylist Voytek Frykowski and Abigail Folger, heiress to the Folger coffee fortune, died alongside her. Their murderers were Tex Watson, Susan Atkins, Linda Kasabian and Patricia Krenwinkel, while the gutless Manson stayed well out of the way. The following night Manson, with six family members, Watson, Atkins, Kasabian and Krenwinkel, were joined by Leslie Van Houten and Steve 'Clem' Grogan. The group went out driving to find other people to kill. They eventually arrived at 3301 Waverly Drive, Los Angeles, the home of supermarket executive Leno LaBianca and his wife, Rosemary, who co-owned a dress shop. Leno and Rosemary were stabbed multiple times then shot to death.

Perhaps the best way to start studying the life and crimes of Manson and his family is to watch *Helter Skelter*, and to completely forget any of the other productions that are allegedly based on these dreadful events.

To fully familiarise yourself with the case this film explores, use Google Maps to find the crime scene locations. You can also watch scores of videotaped interviews with Manson and some of his followers on YouTube. What I wouldn't advise searching for are the post-mortem photos of all of the victims. The beautiful actress, Sharon Tate, 'was gutted like a pig', claimed Krenwinkel, which sums it all up.

Charles Manson died of a heart attack on 19 November 2017. He had been diagnosed with colon cancer some years earlier. His body was cremated with his ashes given to a family friend.

Sharon Marie Tate was aged just twenty-six when Manson's monsters butchered her. She and her unborn baby are buried together, along with her mother, Doris Gwendolyn Tate, and her sister, Patricia Gay Tate, at the Holy Cross Cemetery, Culver City, LA.

The Tate house no longer stands but interest in these senseless murders shows no sign of waning. Three new movies were in production in 2019. Do Manson and his followers deserve the criminal celebrity status they undoubtedly have? Imagine the people who were murdered were your kith and kin and there's your answer.

The Boston Strangler

It could be suggested that this 1968 neo-noir movie does the true-crime inspired film genre a disservice in every sense of the word. Very much like *The Amityville Horror*, this could be described as exploitation, running right below the moral waterline. *The Boston Strangler* does have a star-studded cast. It was nominated for a Golden Globe Award and received two other nominations as ACE (USA) 1969 Best Edited Feature Film, and the Edgar Allan Poe Awards 1969 Best Motion Picture. However, critics came out with mixed reviews. Several, including Roger Ebert, sat on the fence. Rotten Tomatoes gives it 86 per cent, and IMDb handed down 7.1/10. So, this is a film that one likes or one does not like.

It would be fair to say that Tony Curtis who plays Albert Henry DeSalvo gives us a great portrayal of the serial killer. Dubbed by the media 'The Boston Strangler', DeSalvo confessed to the murders of thirteen women, aged between nineteen and eighty-five, in the Boston area between 1962 and 1964. Also starring is Henry Fonda who is fantastic, as is George Kennedy, Sally Kellerman and Jiri Voskovec who plays Peter Hurkos.

One cannot fault the acting at all. But let's look – as we did with *Helter Skelter* and *To Catch a Killer* – at what professional credentials there are to back up this film.

The film is based on a book by the same name written by Gerold Frank (1907-1998), an American author and ghostwriter. Frank penned several celebrity memoirs and was considered a pioneer of the 'as told to' form of autobiography. His two best known books are *The Boston Strangler* (1966), and *An American Death* (1972) concerning the assassination of Martin Luther King. One look at his life and selected works proves that Frank knew his stuff, but where did this 'as told to' form of autobiography originate?

'Autobiography', as we all know, means an account of a person's life written by *that* person – as in 'the first person'. However – and this *is* important – at the time that the real-life DeSalvo was allegedly writing his 'autobiography' he was in jail and making confessions for rape and murder under hypnosis carried out by the distinguished William Joseph Bryan Jr. Of his 'confessions' *none* could be substantiated in pretty much any forensically provable form. So the dates *are* important here, and one might smell a rat simply because, at his 1967 trial, DeSalvo's mental state was evaluated by Dr Harry Kozol, a neurologist who had established the first sex offender treatment centre in Massachusetts. Henry was destined to spend the remainder of his life making confessions then retracting them at the Massachusetts Correctional Institution in Cedar Junction, Walpole, where, aged forty-two, he was murdered in a drugs dispute on 25 November 1973. So we're led to believe Henry DeSalvo wrote his autobiography. I think not. Even the quickest glance through any alleged authoritative account of DeSalvo's life of alleged crime throws up red flags all over the place. To start with, the dates when Henry *might* have written all of this down are out of sync with Frank's alleged 'as told by' claim. Furthermore, there is no mention anywhere, in any place, in any police records, attorney's notes or court papers, that DeSalvo had ever met Gerold Frank. There is nothing in DeSalvo's custodial records that he penned anything other than his signature, let alone received visits from the writer – he'd probably never heard of Frank, either. Yes, DeSalvo probably murdered a couple of people. But did he kill all thirteen victims of the 'Stranger'? I think not.

Around this time the Boston cops were well known to be doing 'Henry Lucas Jobs': pinning unsolved homicides onto saps who were mentally unstable to say the least, and who were mouthing off about being a serial killer when they were nothing of the sort. In a sentence: the cops fitted people up!

As most of us will know, some people are inclined to admit to crimes they have not committed just to gain the attention of the police and media. Most of them are not exactly mentally stable either – well one wouldn't be, right? Nevertheless, back in the sixties, it was very much accepted US police practice to get a confession at *any* cost – even beating the living daylights out of a man. If you were in the frame you stayed in the frame. Cops and District Attorney's careers depended upon crime clear-up rates. Promotion came quickly with the DA, always with his beady eye on being risen to the bench and 'beakship', maybe even to Governor of a state.

On 15 August 2018, Faye Skelton of Edinburgh Napier University cited the case of officer clerk Stefan Kiszko in her article, *Suspects confess to crimes they didn't commit – here's why.* Kiszko spent seventeen years in prison for the murder of eleven-year-old Lesley Molseed, in Rochdale, northwest England, in 1975. Though Kiszko had confessed his guilt to the police at the time, evidence later proved that he was innocent. Faye's article can be found on the internet. One MP described Kiszko's ordeal as: 'The worst miscarriage of justice of all time.' Possibly a bit of an overstatement, nevertheless, evidence that Kiszko could not have committed the crime was suppressed by three leading members of the investigation team, who were arrested in 1993, before the charges were conveniently dropped. A DNA match led to the arrest of Ronald Castree for Lesley's murder. He is now serving a life term in prison.

It is a sad thing to get our heads around, but this sort of corrupt police behaviour has been going on since Sir Robert 'Bobby' Peel invented 'The Peelers' in 1829, later to become 'The Bobbies'. Indeed, I have seen this myself in the case of the aforementioned Joe Odell, and that of the softly spoken William 'Bill' Heirens (1928-2012) who I interviewed many years back for a TV documentary at the Vienna Correctional Centre, in Illinois. I dedicated a chapter to Heirens in my book *Talking with Serial Killers.* During the research for that programme and book I interviewed attorneys for both defence and prosecution and also the trial judge – all of whom had the gall to tell me that it was obvious that Heiren was innocent of murder, but 'politics' and 'promotion' at the time demanded 'justice at any cost'.

And this brings me back to the movie, *The Boston Strangler*. It's true-crime credentials are good-to-go. Yet, under closer scrutiny, using the 'as told by' is disingenuous, thus totally flawed. Still, with that being said, it does make for entertainment of sorts, so on this occasion we can set aside thoughts of cinematic exploitation of the real-life victims and move on.

Zodiac

The real-life Zodiac case has more twists and turns than a hundred snakes in a small wicker basket – thus it was a shoo-in for a decent movie, which it ultimately became. Therefore, if you're looking for something to get your teeth into, this film, tactfully produced by David Fincher, is refreshing in that it spends more time illustrating the nuances of the characters and recreating the mood of the not-so-swinging seventies than in the gory details of murder most foul.

Zodiac (2007) at two hours and forty-two minutes is based on real-life events and a must-watch for true crime buffs, and is based upon Robert Graysmith's excellent 1986 book of the same name.

Born in 1942, Graysmith is a US true crime author and former cartoonist and is to be applauded for his work in trying to solve the case, which is as complicated as any homicidal Rubric puzzle if there ever is/was one. With that being said, Graysmith published *Zodiac Unmasked*: *The Identity of America's Most Elusive Serial Killer Revealed* in 2002, so if you need to know who the Zodiac (a pseudonym for apparently the still unidentified killer) killer was, or may have been, I won't spoil your fun. But take your 'time' watching the film, for somewhat cryptically the answer is something to 'watch' for. There, two not-so-subtle clues already for you.

This wasn't one of Fincher's best films. Nonetheless it portrays a rash of killings that took place during the 1960s and '70s, and the film – as far as Hollywood was concerned – was not a success despite it costing about $60 million to make and only saw returns of half of that despite it starring some of Tinseltown's hottest talents including Jake Gyllenhaal, Mark Ruffalo, Robert Downey Jr, Chloe Sevigny, John Carroll Lynch, Brian Cox and Philip Baker Hall. However, despite the movie's failure at the box office the subject is one that seems to pique the publics' interest whenever it is mentioned.

Earlier in this book we looked a little into Henry Lee Lucas's psychopathology, and this provides some interesting insights into the then unknown media-dubbed 'Zodiac' killer. Thus, when Graysmith consulted forensic psychiatrist, Dr Donald Lunde, Lunde explained that there are two basic types of serial killer: paranoid schizophrenic – suffering from delusions – and sexual sadists. The sadistic serial killer 'selects his victims for the purpose of venting certain deeply rooted sexual and sadistic urges, such as the need to mutilate parts of the victim's body,' says Lunde. And, speaking of the similarity between serial killers Ed Kemper and Kenneth Bianchi, Dr Lunde commented on their similar interest in 'seeing animals torn apart and blood and animal hearts'. Dr Lunde and I debated Bianchi many years ago and in this respect there was never any evidence that Bianchi was ever involved with this type of grisly animalistic behaviour, although he was a sexual sadist and Dr Lunde finally agreed to that. However, in trying to profile the mysterious Zodiac for Graysmith, he did draw the author's attention to the fact that many such serial killers usually have a passive father and a dominant mother, to whom his attitude is a mixture of desire and hatred.

Well, I have been around serial killers for decades now, so I am going to add into this chapter a few YouTube video links, stuff that will truly get your head spinning, and as all of my readers are up for solving crime puzzles – sort of like our loveable Columbo played by the late Peter Falk – why not watch the movie first then follow up on the internet links. Or, if you want to go back to front, then watch the YouTube material first then watch the film. However, whatever way you play this, I am sure that you will come out none-the-wiser.

Now it is killing time, but I will only deal with probably the first two events simply because the Zodiac's victim total is: five confirmed dead; two injured; possibly between twenty and twenty-eight total dead and he claimed to have killed thirty-seven times. So get your head around that if you care to, so here we go.

The time and date: 11 p.m., 20 December 1968. It was a typically chilly, moonlit night in the Vallejo hills overlooking San Francisco. Teenagers David Arthur Faraday, aged seventeen, and his girlfriend, Betty Lou Jensen, sixteen, were parked up at a turn-off on the Lake Herman Road, a well-known and quiet lovers' lane just within the limits of the town of Benicia. Suddenly bullets blasted into Faraday's white Rambler, while another bullet ploughed into the bodywork. Betty, who had never dated before, flung open the passenger door and scrambled out. David tried to follow her when the shooter leaned in through the driver's window and shot him in the head. As Betty ran for her life, the shooter fired five times. She collapsed spread-eagled on her stomach before she had run ten yards. The gunman then calmly walked back to his car and drove away.

As fate would have it, another car drove past the open space by the pump house where the two teens lay. The female driver saw Betty Lou sprawled on the ground, but she did not stop. Instead, she accelerated on towards the town of Benicia and when she saw the blinking lights of a police car coming towards her, she frantically flashed her headlights to attract the cop's attention. When, three minutes later at precisely 11.28 p.m., Captain Daniel Peta and a colleague from the Volusia PD arrived on-scene, they found that David Faraday was still clinging on to life, but Betty was dead. David was to die shortly after his arrival at the Vallejo hospital at 12.05 a.m.

For Detective Sergeant Les Lundblatt of the Vallejo PD, the case was motiveless. David's wallet was intact; Betty had not been sexually assaulted. An investigation into the background of the teenagers ruled out the theory that some jealous rival had shot them; they were ordinary students whose lives were an open book.

Six months later the dead kids had become merely two more statistics in California's huge file of cold case homicides. Then, on 4 July 1969, the killer went hunting again. In a car park only two miles from the place where David and Betty were shot, twenty-two-year-old waitress, Darlene Ferrin, was sitting in a car with her boyfriend, Mike Mageau. The time was just before midnight when a white sedan pulled alongside them; there were several other cars in the park so the driver drove away after a few minutes then returned and parked on the other side. Suddenly a powerful light shone in on them. Assuming it was a police spotlight, Mike reached for his driver's licence. There was an explosion of gunfire, and Darlene collapsed. Moments later, a bullet tore into Mike's neck. The man turned and walked back to his own car, paused to fire another four shots at them, then drove off so fast he left a smell of burning rubber.

'I wish to report a double murder. If you go one mile east on Columbus Parkway to a park you will find the kids in a brown car. They have been shot by a 9mm Luger. I also killed those kids last year. Goodbye.'

The Zodiac, in a phone call to police dispatcher Nancy Slover, at 12.40 a.m. on 5 July 1969. The call was traced to a callbox just a few blocks from the Police Department.

When the police arrived at Blue Rock Park they discovered that the caller had made a mistake: it was not a double murder. Mike Mageau was still alive, although the bullet had passed through his tongue, preventing him from speaking. However, this time there were leads. Four months earlier, Darlene's babysitter had been curious about a white car parked outside Darlene's apartment. When she asked Darlene about it, the waitress replied: 'He's checking up on me again. He doesn't want anyone to know what I saw him do. I saw him murder someone.' She was able to offer a description of the man – round-faced, with brown wavy hair, probably middle-aged. When Mike recovered enough to talk, he described the killer as round-faced with brown wavy hair.

A month later, on 1 August 1969, three local newspapers – the *San Francisco Examiner*, the *San*

Francisco Chronicle and *Vallejo Times Herald* – received handwritten letters which began: 'Dear Editor. This is the murderer of the 2 teenagers last Christmas at lake Herman [*sic*] and the girl on the 4th of July...' it went on to give details of the ammunition which left no doubt the writer was the killer. Actually, the letters were not identical: they were sent in three parts to be combined as a whole and each letter also contained a third sheet of paper containing a message in cipher – the writer claimed it gave his name. He asked that it should be printed on the front page of the newspapers, and threatened that if this was not done, he would go on a killing rampage: '...killing lone people in the night'. The letters were signed with a symbol of a cross within a circle; it looked ominously like a gun sight.

All three letters were published – at least in part – and the texts of the cryptograms were published in full. Code experts from the FBI and at the Mare Island Naval Shipyard tried to crack it – without success. But one man – a schoolteacher from Salinas named Dale Harden – had the inspired idea of looking for groups of signs that might fit the word 'kill'. Harden believed that the killer was ego-driven so they just guess that the first letter would be 'I'. After that, they also assumed the word 'kill' would be in the message, so they looked for the symbol that they assumed was 'i' with two 'l's' next to each other. After that it didn't take longer than ten hours to break the code. In it the Zodiac said:

> *I like killing people because it is so much fun. It is more fun than killing wild game in the forest because man is the most dangerous animal of all. To kill something*

gives me the most thrilling experience, it is even better than getting your rocks off with a girl. The best past is when they die I will be reborn in Paradise and all that I have killed will become my slaves. I will not give you my name because you will try and slow me down or stop my collecting of slaves from my afterlife.

Of further interest, the Zodiac killer appears to have been a movie buff. In one of his ciphers, Zodiac seemed to mention a film called *The Most Dangerous Game* (1932), which is all about a homicidal hunter who plots to wreck a ship on an island, so that he can play his game of hunting down and, yes, of course, killing the hapless passengers. He also called himself 'the Red Phantom' which seems to come from another movie, so look up 'Zodiac Ciphers: Who is the Red Phantom?' on the internet and figure this all out because I cannot.

With that movie trivia out of the way, two months later, on 27 September 1969, a young couple went for a picnic on the shores of Lake Berressa, thirteen miles north of Vallejo. Bryan Hartnell, aged twenty, and Cecelia Ann Shepard, twenty-two, were both students at nearby Pacific Union College, a Seventh Day Adventist institution. They had been lying on a blanket in the warm September sunlight, kissing, then they had eaten.

At about 4.30 p.m., both noticed a man across the clearing; he seemed stockily built and had brown hair. The man vanished into a grove of trees, minutes later emerging again wearing some kind of hooded mask and carrying a gun. As he came closer, they saw that he had a white symbol on the front of the material that hung down from the hood – a circle with a cross inside it.

'I want your money and your car keys,' said the soft voice inside the hood. Hartnell said he was welcome to the 76 cents he had. The man began to talk in a rambling manner, explaining that he was an escaped convict and finally said that he had to tie them up and produced a length of clothesline. They talked for several more minutes, then the man announced: 'I'm going to have to stab you people.'

'Please stab me first,' said Hartnell, 'I couldn't bear to see her stabbed.' 'I'll do just that,' said the assailant calmly. He dropped to his knees and plunged a hunting knife repeatedly into Bryan's back. Sick and dizzy with pain, the student then watched him attack Cecelia. After the first stab, the killer seemed to go berserk; he stabbed her again and again, while she twisted frantically. When she finally lay still, the man walked over to their car, drew something on the door with a felt-tipped pen then walked away.

A fisherman who had heard their screams found the couple soon after. They were both still alive when the Napa Police arrived. They had been alerted by an anonymous telephone call. A man with a gruff voice had told them 'I want to report a double murder' and gave them the precise description of the 'bodies'. He left the phone dangling.

Cecelia Shepard died two days later without recovering from her coma. Bryan Hartnell survived and was able to describe their attacker. The police had already guessed the murderer's modus operandi – his crime signature for the sign on the car door was a circle with a cross in it, and this is where we part company with the Zodiac, or at least we try to.

The great thing about this movie is it's more-or-less based on real life events. It is non-exploitative either with the proviso that any movie based on such an enigmatic unknown serial killer – Jack the Ripper, for example – is going to generate at least some measure of box office success, even though it would never become a blockbuster, which is a great shame if you care to ask me because the case, in its entirety, is a rich layer cake of intrigue and trickery over and over and over again.

Even in the most carefully crafted crime movies, be they factual or fiction, we pretty much know who the main culprit is from the outset – his or her name will head the cast list which is a dead giveaway, please excuse the pun. But with *Zodiac* we are led up the garden path with four Zodiac suspects, and no one gets caught. The point I am making is this: OK, yes, 'Jack the Ripper' may well have been the first ever world-infamous serial killer and he wrote a few cryptic letters too. However, with merely five victims, or so we are led to believe, Zodiac beats the Victorian pants off of our Jack, so at least he deserves some credit for that!

Whether or not Sherlock Holmes or Lt Columbo could have solved the riddle of who the Zodiac actually is/was is a matter for debate. Nevertheless, I think that our modern-day offender profilers would have identified his true identity much sooner than never at all.

But there is still hope and if the reader is criminology-minded, has a need to try and solve perhaps one of the most terrifying homicide riddles of more recent years, this movie and the following YouTube video (the remainder are just tasters with a few half-decent titbits thrown in) may well help you along the way or drive you right up the wall, but all I ask is that you keep a very open mind from start to finish.

'His Name was Arthur Leigh Allen' – full forty-two-minute documentary. But is this really the killer? There is some fascinating material and first-hand accounts in this programme, along with psychological profiling. A must-watch and sweet dreams, too.

The Executioner's Song

There are few things more disaster-prone than the designs of petty criminals who have aspirations above their ability. Influenced by what they read, or see in the movies or on TV, these over-ambitious mediocrities consider that they are capable of emulating the exploits of those whom they perceive to be eminently more successful than they themselves have been. Fuelled by motives like passion, greed or revenge, they lay plans, which are ill-conceived and, almost always, destined to end in failure. Gary Mark Gilmore (1940-1977) is an example of many thousands of mindless thugs who take innocent folk's lives for a derisory few dollars. Gilmore was executed by firing squad at Utah State Prison on Thursday, 17 January 1977.

Gilmore spent most of his adult life in prison, and, when given another chance at the age of thirty-five, he pissed over the trust numerous people gave him when he shot to death a twenty-four-year-old Mormon gas station attendant called Max Jensen for a measly $125 (£112). Shortly thereafter, Gilmore proceeded to blow away a motel clerk called Benny Bushnell for a similar amount of money. These were not remarkable crimes. So how did Gilmore become one of the most infamous killers in cinematic history? If the truth be known it was because a novelist called Norman Mailer who was asked to write Gilmore's story using the hundreds of hours of interviews a freelance film producer called Larry Schiller had collected from all of the participants in this grim case. And what both Schiller and Mailer were about to do was to make a silk purse out of a sow's ear.

Despite his many notable achievements, Lawrence 'Larry' Schiller had acquired a reputation as a hustler and a 'carrion bird' – a journalist specialising in writing about death – largely due to his acquisition of interviews with Jack Ruby, the man who assassinated Lee Harvey Oswald, just before he died. As a boy, Schiller listened to the New York police radio and waited for news of accidents, which he would then cycle to in order to photograph the scenes so he could sell prints to the insurance companies. Bright lad was Larry!

As one of *Life* magazine's youngest photographers, Schiller covered many major news stories of the fifties and sixties, and in 1963 he sold a single nude photo of Marilyn Monroe to *Playboy* for a record fee of $25,000 (£22,000). Later, in the 1960s, he published *Minamata*, exposing mercury poisoning in Japanese waters, and did photographic montage work on several movies, including *Butch Cassidy and the Sundance Kid*. In the seventies, he became a movie producer. His films included *Marilyn*, based on a book of his photos of Monroe that were accompanied by Norman Mailer's text, and *The Man who Skied Down Everest* (1975) which won an Oscar.

To add gravitas to this rather run-of-the-mill double homicide case, Schiller approached world-renowned novelist, Norman Kingsley Mailer (1923-2007). As well as an author, Mailer was a journalist, essayist, playwright, filmmaker, actor and liberal political activist and he threw his considerable expertise into the story. The resulting *The Executioner's Song* became the 1979 winner of the Pulitzer Prize for fiction and is recognised as his best work. It subsequently became a 1982 movie, by the same name, starring Tommy Lee Jones (Gilmore), Rosanna Arquette (Nicole Baker), and Eli Wallach (Uncle Vern).

Aired over two nights on NBC in 1982, Tommy Lee Jones won an Emmy for his searing performance as the wanton killer, Gary Gilmore. The production showed one can take the exploits of a low-life individual who turned to burglary when he was just ten-years-old, was as an adult never out of prison for more than eight months at a stretch, and could ultimately not escape his execution – and make him into some kind of anti-hero.

Perhaps Gilmore's father, Frank, had a better story to tell. Frank was the illegitimate son of vaudeville entertainer, Fay La Foe, whose own father was the entertainer, Erik Weisz – later Harold Weiss – (1874-1926) who found great fame as the escapologist, Harry Houdini. Amongst his breathtaking stunts, he would demonstrate his power to his audience by inviting them to hit him in his flexed stomach muscles, which, to be quite honest with you, is a stupid thing to do. There are various accounts of how Houdini met his end. One theory is that his demise was apparently brought about by a boy who caught him off-guard. A blow from a baseball bat had caused Houdini internal injuries and he died of peritonitis, secondary to a ruptured appendix at 1.26 p.m. on 31 October 1926. Another theory claims that a McGill University student, Jocelyn Gordon Whitehead (1895-1954), repeatedly punched fifty-two-year-old Houdini's abdomen as he reclined on a couch in his dressing room. Whichever is true, Harry is presently now in a completely escape-proof box some six feet under at the Machpelah Cemetery, Ridgewood, Queens County, New York.

Although Gilmore had an escapologist's genes, he could not escape from a carefully aimed firing squad. His body was cremated and the ashes scattered from a light aircraft over Spanish Fork and other parts of the wide-open Utah countryside. Strange world we live in, indeed.

In Cold Blood

Truman Garcia Capote's allegedly true-crime novel of 1966, *In Cold Blood*, became a movie of the same name in 1967. Several of Capote's works are considered as literary classics and include the novella *Breakfast at Tiffany's* (1958). But he has earned everlasting fame after researching and writing about the murders of the Clutter family, in their home in Holcomb, Kansas, on Sunday, 15 November 1959.

Herb Clutter was a well-respected farmer who lived with his wife, Bonnie, and two youngest children, sixteen-year-old Nancy, and Kenyon, then aged fifteen. Along with the rest of the nation, Capote read about the Clutter killings in the newspapers and, intrigued, he travelled to Kansas to begin research on what he would call the first 'non-fiction novel'. The result was the first true crime book in publishing history to become a novel allegedly based on fact.

The city of Holcomb had taken its name from a local hog farmer and, by its very nature 'The Sunflower State' is tall-grass prairie country first settled by the Americans in 1827 with the establishment of Fort Leavenworth.

Here, they grow wheat and lots of it. The Clutters grew wheat. Like so many other remote places, back in the fifties the locals in Holcomb were suspicious of outsiders, but this was heightened when some of their own were slaughtered. Eyebrows were raised when one Truman Capote arrived in town, started knocking on doors and asking damned impertinent questions.

The murders themselves were the result of a robbery. Acting on a tip from a former fellow con called Floyd Wells, who had previously worked for the Clutters, parolees Perry Edward Smith, aged thirty-six, and Richard Hickock, aged thirty-three and the father of three children, drove to the farm in the hope that they would find a safe containing $10,000. There was no such safe. So Smith cut the throat of Herbert Clutter, and then shot him. He then shot Kenyon in the head with a shotgun at close range. It's not clear which man shot Nancy and Bonnie – both men blamed the other. Smith and Hickock were eventually executed by hanging on Wednesday, 14 April 1965.

Let's drill down into Capote's research into his book. Capote wasn't just distilling reality, he was massaging the truth almost to the point of his right hand getting cramp. To start with, he composed accounts that diverged from even his own notes and conjured up entire scenes that had no basis in reality. This is exactly why I have included *In Cold Blood* in this book. It is part of the very reason why I have written it. For Capote, fabricating or otherwise, it is right to suggest that any narrative representation of 'selected' details, and the process of selection and arrangement through which a writer converts disparate facts into an absorbing story, indeed entails an inevitable measure of sacrifice. As Patrick Radden Keefe, writing his piece 'Capote's Co-Conspirators' for *The New Yorker*, 22 March 2013, says: 'Even in the most scrupulously factual (fact-checked) piece of narrative journalism, the writer uses some details and discards others, focuses on some characters and ignores others altogether, withholds information, and then metes it out as it suits him.' Is this a kind of selective amnesia? Is this blatant manipulation or just the desire to write a book that would, as Capote said, 'endure'.

Capote explained that he selected a crime story because 'murder was a theme not likely to darken and yellow with time.' That statement was true then and remains so now. As Keefe rightly points out: 'Some of this persistent interest in the backstory of *In Cold Blood* may simply be a product of its greatness: even detractors who would like to see it plucked from the "True Crime" section and re-shelved in "Fiction" still tend to concede that the book was a major literary achievement.' I wholeheartedly agree. The reader might well enjoy Patrick Keefe's take on Capote. It is brilliantly researched and written with much thought and bipartisan compassion. If one were to be harsh, one could argue that by writing *In Cold Blood*, Truman Capote committed a fraud by convincing his readers that it was based in complete truth. Yes Capote gilded the lily. Yes he massaged truth into fiction. But where does his book sit now? *In Cold Blood*, I would suggest, is a masterful work of 'faction' and, considering the true facts of the Clutter murders, and the era during which they were committed, the book has yet to be equalled.

INVENTION VERSUS FACT

As you are reading this book, I am sure that you will have more than a passing interest in all forms of murder. Perhaps you have a fascination for fictional crime and enjoy slasher or horror movies based on pure invention and seasoned with half-truths. It might also be the case that you have a fondness for true crime documentaries – *CSI* and such programmes. I, myself, have been involved in some of these productions, including *Murder by the Sea* and *Voice of a Serial Killer*. You might also be the sort of person who devours as many true crime books as you can. Whichever angle you are coming from you will have an interest in true crime. For my part, as a criminologist, I would prefer to see a case portrayed as accurately as possible – within the limits of screening time and production budgets, naturally. Anyone can rightly criticise a movie regarding length, content and the cast's acting abilities – it's all about personal preferences – but try and produce any motion picture or TV drama/documentary yourself and see just how difficult this can be.

When Stanley Kubrick was asked if he had ever learned anything about his work from film criticism, he replied, 'No. To see a film once and write a review is an absurdity. Yet very few critics ever see a film twice or write about films from a leisurely, thoughtful perspective. The reviews that distinguish most critics, unfortunately, are those slambang pans which are easy to write and fun to write and absolutely useless. There's not much in a critic showing off how clever he is at writing silly, supercilious gags about something he hates.'

Here, Kubrick is being quite diplomatic – something which Irish poet, Brendan Francis Aiden Behan (1923-1964), was not. Behan said, 'Critics are like eunuchs in a harem: they know how it's done, they've seen it done every day, but they are unable to do it themselves.' Even more scathing of the word of critics was English playwright John Osborne (1929-1994): 'Ask a working writer what he feels about critics is like asking a lamppost what it feels about dogs.' Osborne, an actor as well as a screenwriter, was known for his excoriating prose and intense critical stance towards established social and political norms. He hit the literary jackpot with his 1956 play *Look Back in Anger*, which transformed English theatre. Nice one, John. That stuck it to them, my lad!

When I make my comments, I am not criticising a particular film or TV programme *per se*. Rather I am striving to inform the true crime buff what the failings of each portrayal are and which, in my opinion, are the better films to watch – productions that *will* enhance one's knowledge on any given case. Basically, I hope to advise on how to avoid the bullshit crap.

A year ago, I was giving a talk to raise money for a charity. During the Q&A session a lady raised her hand to tell everyone present – me included – that I was misinformed; the Amityville horror films were *totally* true. She went even further, adding: 'I *have* visited the house and it *is* haunted. Even the people in the street have seen Jodie the pig flying about.' Surprisingly, this lady was a councillor and a former mayor! I also know that there are those who have travelled at great expense to Poth to seek out the location where the Texas chainsaw massacre took place – notwithstanding that the killings never happened in Poth at all.

'Sound opinions are valueless. What matters is who holds them,' said Karl Kraus in *Half-Truths and One-and-a-Half-Truths* (1986). So I get this with the proviso that most of the movies and TV documentaries featured throughout these pages are, in *some way*, based on the terrible murders of innocent people just like you and me, or our beloved next-of-kin. Therefore, if an author wants to turn terrible crimes into works of utter fantasy-driven fiction, or massage the real facts to suit his or her own ends, then they are desecrating the graves of the dead.

In our more enlightened times, we have Wikipedia and a host of other websites that will, *or should*, give the reader a mass of free, valuable information about the killer of your choosing. Furthermore, the World Wide Web contains an absolute treasure trove of detail: offender back-narratives, further links, including which books and articles and professional papers have been written, or movies or TV documentaries have been produced. Even better still, we have YouTube, where one can even watch police interrogations and court hearings. I often talk with criminology students about how exciting technological developments are for their subject. Long gone are the days when our youngsters were content to sit through criminology-related lectures and to be almost 'programmed' to think like 'Prof A' or 'Prof B'. With the available information, students no longer have to rely on lectures biased towards the psychopathology of killers that influence their thinking processes one way or the other. These days, those interested in criminology, in whatever form it takes, want to know a heck of a lot more.

Years ago, I was invited to give a talk at the prestigious Oxford Union. The previous month, former US president Bill Clinton did the same and the month after I appeared, Orenthal 'O. J.' James Simpson, aka 'The Juice', took his place at the lectern. But that evening, after a great dinner, some 250 of the brightest young minds in the UK listened to me – and listen good and proper they certainly did. Then came the questions. Goodness gracious me, every single query was beautifully put by a deeply enquiring mind. That's how hungry our youngsters are today for fact – *not* fiction – and this precisely forms part of the reason why the book you are reading now has come into existence.

Month after month I receive emails and letters sent to me via my publishers and online from equally enquiring minds. These come from young and old, from all walks of life, and all of them are hungry for the facts. In some instances it's because something didn't jibe as they watched one of the Bundy Land movies. Something didn't seem to fit with what they imagined *was* the truth. Of course, I can only give my opinions on what I do know. As all of my loyal readers know, I say it as it is. If there is some ambiguity, let's say that is the case. Period!

With that said, how can one *not* be entertained by the great fictional horror crime novels penned by Stephen King and Thomas Harris? Where would we be without Dean Koontz, the American author whose novels are billed as suspense thrillers but frequently incorporate elements of horror, fantasy, science fiction, mystery and satire? Although these writers *do* draw upon some factual case materials as background detail (and all writers have to do this whatever the genre) this is *non-exploitive literature* purely designed to be 'entertaining' or to provide a few sleepless nights.

For decades, the book and movie industry have made thriving trade out of the case of Dr Crippen. An American homeopath, ear and eye specialist and dispenser of medicines, Dr Hawley Harvey Crippen (1862-1910), was hanged at HMP Pentonville, London, for the murder of his wife, Cora Henrietta Crippen (1873-1910). After he had poisoned her, he dismembered her remains, wrapped the cadaver up in pyjamas bought from Selby's department store in nearby Holloway Road, and buried her limbless, headless corpse in the cellar of his house at 39 Hilldrop Crescent – a moronically stupid thing to do as we have seen in an earlier chapter where other killers have interred their victims at their home.

The *Islington Gazette* at the time reported the incident as follows:

Hilldrop Crescent is a quiet suburban place, although in the inner ring of the Metropolis, and reasoning specifically, it would be the last spot one would dream of for the scene of a sordid murder. Here it was – in this unlikely quarter – that the corpse of a beautiful woman was dug up.

Here it was that detectives silently came and went; here came eminent professors and official photographers and here came a coffin to bear ways a woman's mangled remains.

It may have well been the case that Cora, a one-time actress, had been beautiful in her prime, but her once good looks and figure had long abandoned her. She was also not loyal and was having affair after affair. She was a nagging bag of wind who did everything to make her loyal spouse's life an abject misery, so the doctor started (quite rightly) having an affair himself with his secretary, a quite tasty, slim lass called Ethel 'Le Neve' Neave. Cora was then about thirty-seven and getting fatter by the week. Crippen was then aged about forty-eight. Petite Ethel had just turned twenty-seven.

But more than just the murder itself, it was Crippen's escape across the Atlantic with his mistress, who had dressed as a boy, and the subsequent police chase that captured the imagination of the public worldwide. He was apprehended in Canada and said to be the first man caught via wireless telegraph when the captain of the *Montrose*, the ship they were on, recognised the pair from their police descriptions. Captain Henry George Kendall had the telegraphist send a wireless telegram to the British authorities: 'Have strong suspicions that Crippen London cellar murderer and accomplice are among saloon passengers. Moustache taken off growing beard. Accomplice dressed as a boy. Manner and build undoubtedly a girl.'

Thirty-seven books have been written about the case (and more will undoubtedly follow) plus a number of plays and a musical, too. Crippen's lover, Ethel Le Neve, got in on the act by selling her story to *Lloyd's Weekly News*. The first instalment appeared on 6 November 1910. The collected story was later published as a book. If you *can* get access to Crippen's display at Scotland Yard's Crime Museum, known as the 'Black Museum', you can see the *real* spade Inspector Dew used to dig up the decomposing body of Cora. There have been two films – including *Dr. Crippen* (1962) starring Donald Pleasence with James Robertson Justice where Mrs Crippen is misnamed as 'Coral' – it was 'Cora' for heaven's sake. We can dismiss that movie out of hand. In my opinion the best documentary would be *The London Cellar Murder of 1910 (Dr. Crippen)*. At twenty-six minutes and available online, it is brilliant.

Even today, allegedly dark mysteries about Crippen remain. Islington Council knocked down 39 Hilldrop Crescent, with its grisly secrets, in 1951 and built Margaret Bondfield House – a block of flats – on the site. Since then, residents have complained of spooky goings-on, sightings that continue to this very day.

It's creepy. When my mum moved in here I came and helped her sort everything out. While we were doing it, we saw a shadow move past the front room window. It was wearing a black hat and had a cape, really old fashioned. We ran out but no one was there. It was awful.

Just the other week I was in bed when I heard this 'knock, knock, knock' at the window. It wasn't the bedroom window, it was somewhere else in the house.

I couldn't just lie there, I went to look around, but there was no one there. It's frightening when you're on your own, but you get used to it. You just have to get on, don't you?

Anne Heathfield (seventy-one): Jon Dean, *Islington Gazette*, 28 December 2014.

Although in a completely different genre, how can we forget *The Ladykillers* (1955)? This was Peter Sellers' first major role in a film in which he has to compete for the attention of Sir Alec Guinness's false teeth as he plays fedora-wearing Professor Marcus. Herbert Lom, Cecil Parker, Jack Warner, Philip Stainton, Danny Green and the scene-stealing Katie Johnson as the gullible old lady they are trying to kill all star. Filmed in black and white, this is true British crime comedy at its tongue-in-cheek best. It provides atmosphere, tone, and visually stark contrasts capturing the grey, dismal railway-themed production perfectly. It's certainly a film for anyone interested in trains. I'm sure I spotted a 5 LMS Stanier Class 'Black 5' 4-6-0, or maybe it was a 999 BR 'Standard', with its tapered boiler, high running plates, two cylinders and streamlined cab. Who knows?

The interesting thing is that this movie was based on a factual case: a bunch of bungling robbers trying to make off with a suitcase full of cash. Of course, there had to be a remake. The 2004 film of the same name, starring Tom Hanks playing 'The Professor', cannot compete one iota with the original production – and who would want it to? In the same way that the film *10 Rillington Place* was superior, remakes rarely outdo the originals. I mean, how can the admittedly brilliant American actor Tom Hanks compete with Sir Alec Guinness when cast in a film set back in the British fifties? As plots go, as far as railways go, the crime writer's inspiration *has* to come from somewhere, and this, in itself, has a rich pedigree, all providing fertile pickings for creativeness all round, and this further applies to almost every single real-life case, even if it does comes from the Bible, as with *Seven*, for the annals of criminal jurisprudence exhibit human nature in a variety of positions, at once the most striking, interesting and affecting.

Trains, *yes* trains. The 1974 film, *Murder on the Orient Express*, stars Albert Finney, Lauren Bacall, Martin Balsam, Ingrid Bergman, Jacqueline Bisset, Jean-Pierre Cassel, Sean Connery, Sir John Gielgud, Wendy Hiller, Anthony Perkins, Vanessa Redgrave, Rachel Roberts, Richard Widmark and Michael York. So how did the character of Hercule Poirot come about? Did Agatha Christie invent him out of thin air? Of course not. Christie was purposely vague about Poirot's origins, but such a detective was active in the Brussels police force circa 1893.

Nonetheless, the glamour and richly embroidered history of the Orient Express has also been the setting for other plots in literature. In *Dracula* (1897) by Bram Stoker, whilst Count Dracula escapes from England to Varna by sea, the cabal sworn to destroy him travels to Paris and takes the Orient Express, arriving in Varna ahead of him. *Stamboul Train* (1932) by Graham Greene, *Have You Got Everything You Want?* (1933) by Dame Agatha Christie, and *Orient Express* (1934), a novel by Dutch novelist A. den Doolaard also all feature the iconic train. Paul Theroux devotes a chapter of *The Great Railway Bazaar* to his journey from Paris to Istanbul on the Direct-Orient Express. *From Russia, with Love* (1957), the James Bond novel, features the train which writer Ian Fleming had travelled on.

For my part, I have never travelled on the Orient Express. I think that the nearest I have gotten to that sort of long-distance trip via rail are the snow-bound ones from Samara, in Orenburgskaya Oblast, to Moscow. But there's no chance of mystery or murder most foul, fine cuisine, rampant sex or much else on those journeys. I can testify to that. *From Russia, with Love* is not real life. Russian rail travel involves green uniformed, stern-faced *provodniks* with their samovars hissing away, AK-46-toting guards rudely prodding you awake with the gun muzzles to see your ID, fellow passengers trying to be hospitable by offering you in-carriage cooked food one would not feed to a starving dog, and to cap it all one has to crap through a hole in the floor. It makes first-class rail travel in Russia a unique experience indeed.

*

The French novelist and playwright Balzac (1799-1850) called his huge number of novels the 'Human Comedy'. We find this idea being played out in many types of crime movies and TV dramas. I would say that many are tragi-comedies – stories varied by every conceivable change of scene of circumstance. They ring the changes on tragedy, comedy, pathos, passion. In some of the movies in this book, characters are wilfully raised to epic proportions by the need, and the greed, to cinematically feed like vultures on the most awful crimes in history without consideration. But, if we are to subscribe to this, let's make it as factual as possible and not piss over the graves of the dead. I would challenge the reader to find any single character, or plot, in *any* true crime, or fictional book or movie, that does not echo the past. Call it 'plot/character/copycatting'.

When we talk about *real* lady killers, we can hark back to the French serial killer, Henri Desire Landru (1869-1922), aka 'The Bluebeard of Gambais'; dark, bearded, sinister, urbane, the greatest 'lady killer', in the most terrible sense, 'of all time', as writer H. Russell Wakefield says. The movie *Bluebeard* (1972) stars Richard Burton, Raquel Welch, Joey Heatherton and Sybil Danning, but the plot is as far from reality as can be. In fact, there are so many movies, even a Korean film by the same name, that altogether it does the greatest lady killer of all time a great disservice, for this would be enough to turn his blue beard white.

We should also think about the English burglar and murderer, Charles Peace (1832-1879), aka 'The Devil Man', who in barbarous times *might* have been a chieftain, yet civilisation judged his banditry and murders differently. *The Case of Charles Peace* (1949) is too stiff and stodgy to rise above the routine, despite an impish performance by Michael Martin Harvey as the pitiless Peace. And what about the French Pierre Francois Lacenaire (1803-1836), aka 'The Man of Letters'? A social outcast and unsuccessful poet, Lacenaire killed coldly and deliberately for a living, like so many serial killers of more recent times.

The name of portly, pious Dr John Bodkin Adams (1899-1983) will be of special interest for those who might hold suspicions about their own GP. A convicted fraudster and suspected serial killer, between 1946 and 1956, around 163 of his patients died whilst in comas. A must-watch will be the 1986 TV movie, *The Good Doctor Bodkin Adams*. The film stars Timothy West as Dr John Bodkin Adams, and Nigel Davenport as Detective Superintendent Herbert Wheeler Walter Hannam, aka 'Hannam of the Yard'. The reviews were not so hot, *but* from a criminologist's angle this film hits all the right buttons. The locations are spot on, bringing the southeast coastal town of Eastbourne, with its Victorian hotels, the pier and its B&Bs, to life. One can almost smell the sea. Dudley Simpson's incidental music is excellent. And the film includes a lot of stuff on forensics, culminating in a capital murder trial at the central criminal court, the Old Bailey, presided over by Mr Justice Devlin. It turns what could *never* have been a bleak film into something quite remarkable. *The Good Doctor Bodkin Adams* was nominated for the British Academy TV Award for Best Single Drama.

Another home-grown serial killer, Dr Harold Frederick Shipman (1946-2004), springs readily to our minds these days. I take the reader back to this book's dedication and offer congratulations to the filmmakers and cast of *Harold Shipman: Doctor Death* (2002). This sympathetic and well balanced made-for-TV drama was released just two years *after* Shipman was found guilty on all counts, and two years *before* he hanged himself at HMP Wakefield. This would have been a very sensitive time for the literally hundreds of his victims' next-of-kin, the police, and the thousands of residents of the Tameside town of Hyde. Even more so for the scores of trusting patients at the Donneybrook surgery who had believed that the good doctor was the bee's knees. When your doctor is unmasked as the most prolific serial murderer in British history, with perhaps up to 250 kills, that can be a shock.

I have contributed to a TV documentary on Shipman, and I have written about him, and to my mind this is one of the best films in the filmology/criminology genre to have ever been produced. James Bolam is perfectly cast as Dr Shipman; the late James Hazeldine plays DI Stan Egerton, with Gareth Thomas as Reverend Dennis Thomas.

Ever since *Harold Shipman: Doctor Death* was released in 2002 to the present day, this film is a stark reminder for everyone that the medical profession needs to be kept on its toes. I highly recommend that everyone watches it. The final scene (which I will not elaborate upon so as not to spoil your take) says everything – out with the tissues, please.

SOME OF THE BEST

For me to try and bring this book to some form of conclusion is not an easy task. I will leave you on a happy note with what I consider to be some of the best films from both sides of the pond.

Trainspotting (1996):

> *This film does not glorify drugs it glorifies film.*
> Neil Jeffries, *Empire*

It would be hard to imagine a motion picture about drugs, depravity, and all-round bad behaviour more electrifying, yet based upon multiple real-life characters and happenings knitted together, yet non-exploitative than *Trainspotting*. It is, of course, directed by Danny Boyle, his magnum opus starring Ewan McGregor, Jonny Lee Miller, the fantastic Robert Carlyle, Ewen Bremner, and Kelly Macdonald, amongst others. As Kelly Kessler writes in *Common Sense Media*: 'For a unique, consummately entertaining, and yet utterly harrowing look into the life of heroin addicts, this movie offers open-minded viewers an unforgettable experience.' Then we might also refer the filmographies of these actors such as Ewen Bremner in *Black Hawk Down* (2001) playing 'Nelson' alongside Tom Sizemore, William Fichtner, Sam Shepard, Orlando Bloom, Tom Hardy CBE (his debut film), Ewan McGregor, Josh Hartnett and Eric Bana. Therefore, when one watches a movie such as *Trainspotting*, you will know that the research is cinematic perfection; as far as fiction based on lots of real-life social facts go, here you have a belter.

No Country for Old Men (2007):
This is one-hundred-and-twenty-three minutes of violent, poetic, gripping, thrilling and blackly funny cinema. Critic Cynthia Fuchs wrote about *No Country for Old Men*, saying, 'The desolate landscape and moral layout evoke old Westerns, but the film also considers that genre's conventions, suggesting comparisons between now and the old times.' The film plot is not entirely unique. In this film a hunter discovers two million dollars while strolling through the aftermath of a drug deal. To his shock and horror he learns that he is being pursued by a psychopathic killer who, as might be expected, wants the cash back. There is an incredibly talented cast of actors including Tommy Lee Jones, Woody Harrelson, Barry Corbin, Stephen Root, Beth Grant, Javier Bardem and Josh Brolin.

I say that the plot is 'not entirely unique' because in *all* movies where some form of crime is involved there is always a 'catch 'em' theme running throughout. It is always 'cop chases the crooks', or 'mafia-types chasing other mobsters', or the 'sheriff and posse after the bandits'. We see it in the made-for-TV series like *The Sweeney*, *Columbo* or *Miss Marple* as well as throughout silver screen productions, such as: *The Sweeney*, *The Pink Panther*, *The Silence of the Lambs* and *To Catch a Killer*. This is all part of our rich film heritage simply because this all happens in real life. It is embedded in our DNA. Somewhat interestingly, we often want to see the baddies get away and run free because many of us love to see the law outwitted and the tables turned. For example, in the film *Lawless* (2012), Tom Hardy, playing Forrest, turns the tables on the FBI. This motion picture was based on the historical novel *The Wettest County in the World* by Matt Bondurant. Bondurant was, in turn, inspired by his paternal grandfather, Jack, and two grand-uncles, Forrest and Howard. His novel focuses on the events of the 'Great Franklin County Moonshine Conspiracy' – events that ended in a trial related to the illegal activities of the moonshiners in Franklin County, located in the Blue Ridge foothills of the 'Old Dominion State' of Virginia.

American Hustle (2013):

This film has a star-studded cast, with names such as Christian Bale, Jack Huston, Robert De Niro and Jeremy Renner. But the movie appears to be more about Amy Adams' cleavage. The movie stylishly riffs on the FBI's 1970s ABSCAM (sometimes written Abscam) sting operation and is filled with many twists and double-crossings. It is based upon the 1991 book *The Sting Man* written by Robert W. Greene Sr (1929-2008), which won the Edgar Award for Best Fact Crime. This sting operation in the late 1970s and early 1980s led to the convictions of seven members of the United

States Congress, among others. *American Hustle* and the book, *The Sting Man*, are a must-watch-must-read for aficionados of true crime.

Catch Me If You Can (2002):
This may not Steven Spielberg's best motion picture yet it ranks amongst the director's more entertaining ones. It tracks Frank Abagnale's rise as a wunderkind conman. Leonardo DiCaprio has never been more enjoyably charming and slimy at once. Frank William Abagnale Jr is presently an American security consultant who is internationally known for his career between the age of fifteen and twenty-one as a conman, cheque forger and imposter. It stars Tom Hanks, Christopher Walken, Amy Adams, Martin Sheen, James Brolin, Jennifer Garner, and makes for a fascinating study of one of the most duplicitous yet almost loveable conmen of modern times – all of which somewhat reminds me of the historic 'The Great Bank Forgery' of 1873 with George MacDonald and brothers Austin and George Bidwell against a mighty system, and the tiny detail that turned success into failure. And it does come down to something when the sheet anchor of financial security in Great Britain, the Bank of England, got conned, too!

The Wolf of Wall Street (2013):
Hits the spot! The best and boldest thing about this movie, possibly Martin Scorsese's most focused, indulgent movie, is how fun it makes its crime look. Scorsese and writer Terence Winter condense fraudulent stockbroker Jordon Belfort's memoir down to basically the most component and sensational parts, putting you into the

mind of a young man who sees other people's money as his own. Lots of sex and drug-soaked comedy, with Leonardo DiCaprio and supporting cast taking real crime into three hours of perfectly adapted cinema.

Yet, here again, frauds similar to Belfort's date back generations and, off the top of my head I refer to the gigantic frauds committed by British Liberal Party politician Jabez Balfour: bogus building societies, guinea-pig directors, demonstrations of philanthropy and piety – Jabez Balfour (1843–1916) knew all the ways of deceiving others and of helping himself.

Casino (1995):
Scorsese slams another cracker in with this somewhat underrated 1990s gangster effort living in the shadow of *Goodfellas*. Once again we have Robert De Niro as a low-level mobster making his way up the casino racket (based on the real-life Frank Lawrence 'Lefty' Rosenthal), the delicious Sharon Stone and enforcer Joe Pesci as the wife and friend who threaten to tear everything down. Joe Pesci (whose character Nicky Santoro is based on real-life mobster Anthony Spilotro), Sharon Stone, Don Rickles, James Woods, Frank Vincent, L.Q. Jones and the other players are shoo-ins performing their parts to perfection. Rosenthal (1929-2008) was a professional sports better, former Las Vegas casino executive and organised crime associate. His story alone makes for fascinating study.

Dog Day Afternoon (1975):
I have doubts about this film although it was inspired by a real-life robbery that took place on 22 August 1972

at a Chase Manhattan branch in Gravesend, Brooklyn. This neo-noir movie solidified Al Pacino's legend, in all its spittle-filled, shouting glory. Directed by Sidney Lumet and fuelled by a gripping performance from Pacino, the film offers a finely detailed snapshot of people in crisis with tension-soaked drama, all lightened occasionally with black humour. Of course the plot – the robbing of a bank – is common enough in the annals of criminal history. It's what Bonnie and Clyde did, and what hundreds more villains before and after them have done. This robbery has a back story though. The film is based on the real-life case of John Wojtowicz, a twenty-seven-year-old married man from Brooklyn. Also a Vietnam veteran, Wojtowicz had a stream of gay lovers on the side, and he decided to embark upon a Mickey Mouse scheme to rob a bank in order to pay for a lover's sex change. A fourteen-hour hostage siege ensued – 'one that riveted the nation' as the *New York Post* reported. While Wojtowicz's portrayal on film became the stuff of legend, the man himself remained little heard of until his death, after which a documentary, *The Dog*, hit the theatres.

There is a twist – one which proves that what happens in real life can be far more outlandish than any movie. It is no wonder that some of the real details didn't make it to the big screen. In fact, if the truth had been known, I don't think that many respected actors would have entertained casting at all. The night before the robbery, Wojtowicz and his accomplices – eighteen-year-old Sal Naturale and twenty-year-old Bobby Westenberg – stayed in a New Jersey hotel. Wojtowicz had agreed to pay Westenberg $50,000 for his assistance, but for that money Wojtowicz wanted more than just a partner in crime. This self-described 'pervert' had ironically met his wife, Carmen, at a bank where they both worked in the mid-sixties. Wojtowicz was drafted soon after and had his first homosexual experience during basic training. After serving in Vietnam (still married to Carmen) Wojtowicz joined the Gay Activists Alliance (GAA) – where he was known as a 'Looney-tune guy' – but was driven more by a desire for sex than politics. 'He was a disgrace. He would fall on a couch and start having sex in a semi-public place,' said journalist Randy Wicker, who helped Wojtowicz negotiate the film rights to his story.

I won't labour further on Wojtowicz's unedifying behaviour because it goes from bad to worse. The robbery turned into a fourteen-hour circus that had over two thousand onlookers on the scene rooting for him. At one point, Wojtowicz threw money out to the crowd. Naturale was shot dead by the FBI and Wojtowicz got a mere five years in prison. He died of cancer in 2006. Wicker observes of the film that 'They [the filmmakers and the actors] had no real understanding that John Wojtowicz was as crazy as he was. He comes out more rational than he really was.' It all somewhat proves that even though this film received excellent reviews – most likely because the critics were unaware of the true nature of John Wojtowicz's back history – one can still make a silk purse out of a sow's ear.

The French Connection (1971):
Undoubtedly one of my favourite real-life criminal events ever to have been so beautifully put onto the

silver screen. The much-loved Gene Hackman gives us yet another cop-chase baddie role, which is totally believable, his sobering performance ending with much moral weight.

All the President's Men (1976):
This is a movie that Donald Trump – at the time of writing the President of the United States – might heed all too well. Robert Redford and Dustin Hoffman made journalism sexy by embodying Bob Woodward and Carl Bernstein as they followed trails that led them to connect a Watergate burglary to President Nixon. History does have a habit of repeating itself!

JFK (1991):
While the assassination of John F. Kennedy remains 'officially' unsolved, Oliver Stone's historical drama is such a persuasive conspiracy thriller that it will leave you convinced that something else was at work – which undoubtedly it was. It's true that *JFK* is a must-watch movie for Kennedy fans and the tens of thousands of conspiracists that debate the case morning, noon and night, but at the end of the day it is simply that: a persuasive conspiracy thriller – nothing more, nothing less – but one with a production budget of $40 million and turning in, at the time of writing, over $200 million in box office receipts, it was odds-on that it was to become a winner.

Parkland (2013):
Directed by Peter Landesman, with a production budget of just $10 million and scraping box office receipts of

$1.6 million, on paper, the maths dictate *Parkland* (the hospital where Kennedy was pronounced dead) was a mega flop despite flawless acting by all of the cast – Billy Bob Thornton, Marcia Gay Harden, and Colin Hanks (Tom's son' well, Tom Hanks was one of the producers after all). The film has, too often unfairly, had to measure itself up to *JFK* – the so-called Gold Standard motion picture on President Kennedy's killing.

Yet *Parkland* doesn't pretend to be a low-budget rip-off of *JFK*, not if co-producers Tom Hanks and Bill Paxton had anything to with it, I'm sure of that. 'Tis true, this is one gritty film, perhaps over-gory at times, but it is, I think, a must-watch, so enjoy it for what it is – sick bags at the ready!

Anatomy of a Murder (1959):
This film has Jimmy Stewart wavering between the comic and the dramatic. The film also stars George C. Scott, the flirtatious and beautiful Lee Remick, Ben Gazzara and Brooks West.

This is an Otto Preminger directed courtroom drama, based on a novel written by a defence attorney and inspired by one of his real-life cases. Michigan Supreme Court Justice, John D. Voelker, wrote under the pen name 'Robert Traver'. Voelker based the novel on a 1952 murder case in which he was the defence attorney. Few movies seem to grasp the moral ambiguity of the US legal system while also being both realistic and tense. In 2012, the film was selected for preservation in the United States National Film Registry by the Library of Congress as being 'culturally, historically, or aesthetically significant'.

M (1931):

This is a film for everyone fascinated by serial homicide and it owes much to German director Friedrich Christian Anton 'Fritz' Lang (1890-1976). The plot revolves around the murders in Germany and a Berlin criminal investigator called Otto Wernicke. Portraying an underworld of criminals who are out to catch one of their own in a murky film noir, it is as scary and thrilling as anything, in my opinion, ever released till this very day.

Dubbed by the British Film Institute, 'The Master of Darkness', Lang's *M* (*M – Eine Stadt sucht einen Mörder* in German) presents a city searching for a serial killer of children. It stars Peter Lorre as Hans Beckert. *M* was Lorre's first major starring role, and it boosted his career.

So, with 'The Master of Darkness' bringing us to the end of this book, does anyone fancy a couple of drinks down the Blind Beggar pub on Whitechapel Road, and where 'Good 'Ole Boy' Ronnie Kray popped a bullet into loudmouth George Cornell's head, then maybe a late night Ruby Murray at The Oriental Indian Express, where you can see lots of flock wallpaper and get sitar-induced tinnitus – it's on our way home.